FURNITU ARRANG—

IN RESIDENTIAL SPACES

V. Asaroglou & A. Bonarou

A step by step guide on how to make a furniture plan that works

All numeric data is given in both metric and imperial units

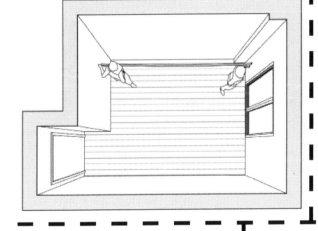

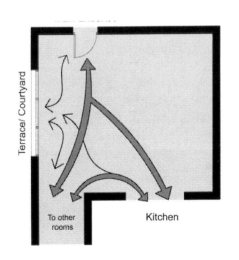

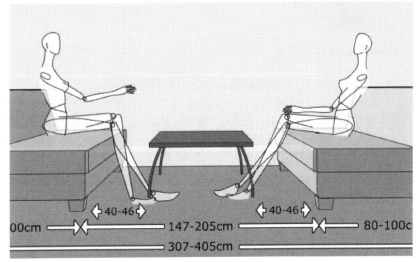

||||||||||||||||||||||||||||||||||||||||||||||||||||||||||||||||||||||||||||||||||||||||||||

Authored & published in 2013 by Anna Bonarou & Vasiliki Asaroglou
Thessaloniki
Greece

||||||||||||||||||||||||||||||||||||||||||||||||||||||||||||||||||||||||||||||||||||||||||

FURNITURE
ARRANGEMENT
IN RESIDENTIAL SPACES

V . A s a r o g l o u
A . B o n a r o u

Preface

The proper furniture placement is one of the most daunting -yet most important- design decisions. Rearranging furniture and/or replacing some pieces with others more suitable can personalize and completely change spaces. No matter whether a room is big or small, narrow or square, the correct furniture arrangement will make it more pleasurable and functional.

Let's assume that you are moving into a new house. One of the first things to consider is the arrangement of the furniture in the provided space. You may decide whether to keep your existing furniture or purchase a few new pieces within your budget.

If you are planning to reuse existing furniture, you have the advantage of knowing the form, style and exact measurements of every piece. The drawback is that some pieces of furniture will be difficult to fit into the new room because of their size (they might be too-small or too-large) or their shape. If you are planning to purchase new furniture, the benefit is that you have more options and greater flexibility. In this case, the disadvantage is that the process of arranging furniture will be more complicated and time consuming, since you won't know the exact measurements and shape of each item in advance.

Rearrange your furniture - Rearrange your life

The long term residence in an abiding space may limit your imagination when it comes to living in an alternatively arranged space.

However, have you ever thought that the environment that surrounds you impacts your habits and daily activities? For example, there is that one book you've always wanted to finish, but you had neither the time nor a proper place at your house to do so. What if you created a cosy and relaxing corner with a comfortable chaise longue and a bookcase? Maybe this will motivate you to start indulging in that book again.

The truth is that one of the easiest low budget changes you can make in order to refresh your home and your life is to simply rearrange your furniture.

Take a look at the conversation area in your living room. Could you make any changes in order to become more inviting and cosy? Look at the overall space available to you. Do you think that you could somehow save some space to create the hobby area that you always wanted or provide additional storage space for you family?

This book offers you all the necessary information you always need but can never find. In the pages of this book, you will find step-by-step instructions to make a furnishing plan that really works. Although the book begins from scratch and explains thoroughly how to measure a room and make a rough sketch, it is also useful to professional interior designers and architects. In fact this book covers all the fundamental principles that relate to furniture arrangement in residential spaces, such as measurements and clearances, circulation paths, ergonomics, furniture grouping, etc.

All numeric data is given in both metric and imperial units.

Vasiliki Asaroglou & Anna Bonarou

CONTENTS

A brief overview of what the book covers

Chapter 1: Measure your space

In the first chapter, you will learn how to make a rough floor plan sketch of your space, how to measure the room and write these measurements down on the sketch. In addition to measuring the overall measurements, you will also learn the importance of measuring other architectural elements, such as doors and windows, fireplaces, built-in elements, etc.

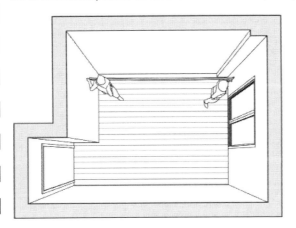 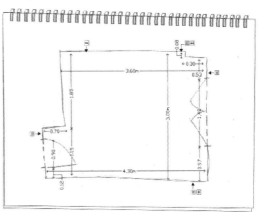

Chapter 2: Draw a floor plan to scale

In the second chapter, you will learn how to draw a scale floor plan on graph paper using the measurements you have made. You will also learn how to make scale furniture cutouts and experiment with different furniture arrangements.

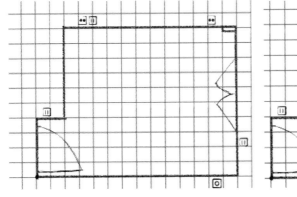 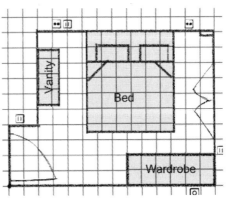

Chapter 3: Analyse space characteristics

In this chapter, you will reflect on your own needs, preferences, activities in a certain space, way of living, number of users, etc and what furniture you will need. You will learn about the four main criteria that affect furniture arrangement: circulation, functions, focal points, and room proportions; the first two are strongly depended on the human factor. More specifically, you will learn how to define circulation paths and ensure that these paths will be wide enough to allow comfortable passage. You will learn how to map functional zones and identify the focal points of a space that respond to your activities and lifestyle. Finally, an example of how to furnish two spaces of the same floor area but different proportions will be really helpful.

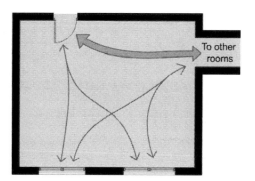
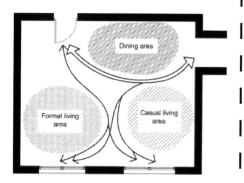

Chapter 4: Arrange the living room

This chapter presents the most common types of seating furniture with measurements, as well as information about the necessary clearances around sofas and coffee tables, the optimum distances, the width of circulation paths between sofas, etc. You will find types of furniture layouts and guidelines for almost every possible way of furniture arranging in the seating area. Finally, you will get information about various TV placements.

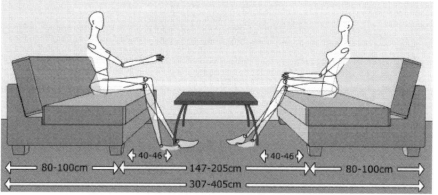
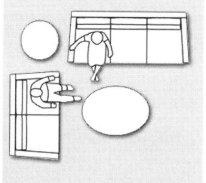

Chapter 5: Arrange the dining room

This chapter categorizes dining tables according to their shape and number of seaters and includes basic measurements, as well as information about clearances around chairs and tables.

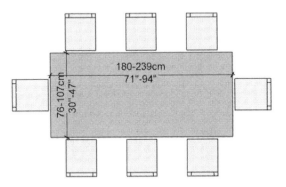

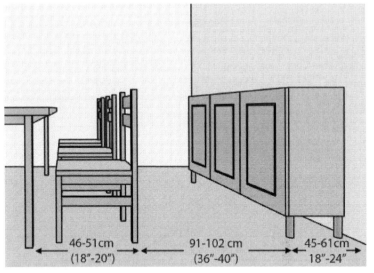

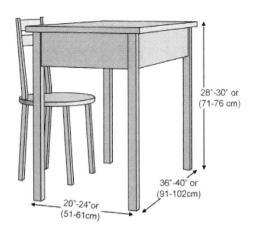

Chapter 6: Storage and study furniture

This chapter presents the most common storage and study pieces of furniture with measurements; the required clearances in front of each piece are also addressed here.

Chapter 7: How to arrange artwork on the walls

This chapter shows almost every alternative of arranging artwork in the living room (mainly above the sofas) and in the bedroom (mainly above the bed headboard).

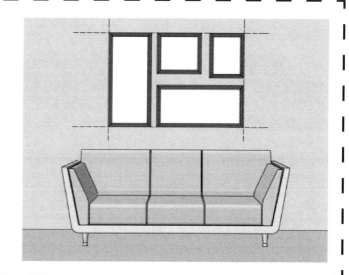

Chapter 8: Arrange the bedroom

This chapter describes the most common types of bedroom furniture with measurements, as well as information about clearances, walking paths widths within a bedroom or a walk-in closet, etc. You will get information about different types of bedrooms, functional zones in each type and guidelines for proper furniture layout in every type of bedroom.

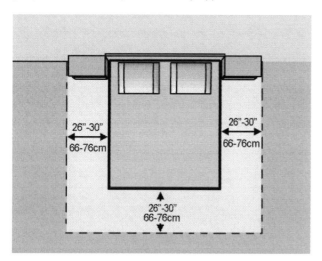

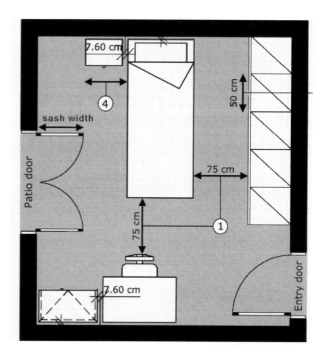

----

1. INTERIOR SPACE
MEASUREMENTS

1. Interior Space measurements

Before you start buying new furnishings or rearranging the existing ones, it is absolutely necessary to measure the available space and write down the overall measurements. Apart from the overall measurements you will need to measure and write down the position and size of secondary architectural elements, such as the doors and the windows, the nooks, the fireplace, etc.

In this chapter you will learn:

- How to make the preliminary observation of the room
- How to sketch out a rough floor plan
- How to take the overall measurements of the room
- How to measure secondary architectural elements
- How to write down the measurements on the sketch
- How to add useful architectural symbols

What is a floor plan?

A floor plan is perhaps the most fundamental architectural drawing that depicts the room as seen from above. A typical floor plan of a room includes
- The shape of the room
- The overall measurements
- The position and size of every architectural element (doors, windows, fireplaces, division walls, etc)
- Any built-in elements, such as wardrobes, radiators, etc

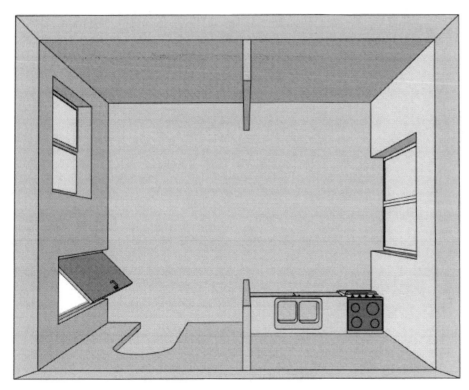

Observe carefully the perspective view of the room and then look at the drawing on the next page. Note that the drawing is actually the floor plan of the particular space.

The floor plan represents accurately the shape of the room, its proportions, the position and size of the doors and windows, etc. The architectural drawings are normally drawn at a scale of 1:50 (metric system) or at a scale of 1/4''=1'-0 (imperial system). Drawing the floor plan at a scale is not enough. It is also necessary to include dimensions in either metric (meters, centimeters, millimeters) or imperial system (inches, feet).

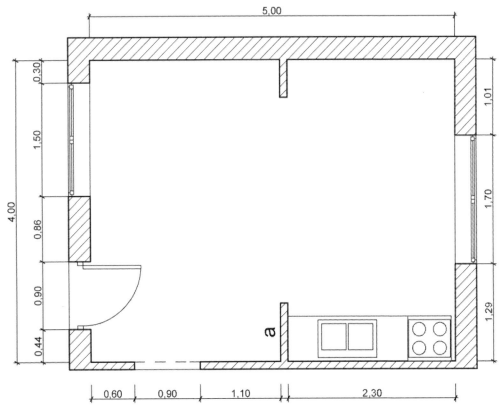

Quiz:
The floor plan is at a scale of 1:50. What is the real life length of the wall "a"?

How to find the wall length: Measure with a ruler the length of the wall on the drawing. Multiply the measurement by fifty and you will find the actual length.

One room, many solutions...

Furniture arrangement is not a problem with one solution. Usually, for every space there are many layouts and each has its strengths and weaknesses. Some solutions are more functional while others are more aesthetically pleasing. In some cases we might decide a rearrangement just to change our daily routine.

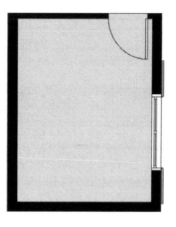

A typical room without furniture

The particular floor plan shows a typical teenager's room. You will need a study area, a single bed, a wardrobe and other smaller pieces of furniture.

There are many criteria you should consider before your final layout, such as the location of the entrance door, the balcony door, the need for natural light, even the location of the switches. However, the most important factor is the overall dimensions of the room.

Possible Layouts

Now look at some possible layouts with the same pieces of furniture. Which one would you choose and why? Can you think of another layout?

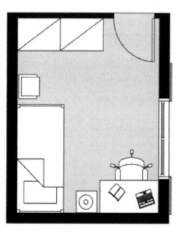
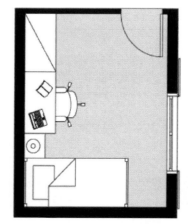
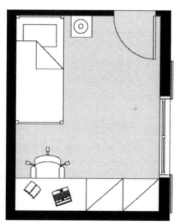

Why do you need to measure the room?

In order to experiment with alternative furniture arrangements you will need to draw a floor plan at a scale. On the architectural drawings, architects and designers experiment with several layouts and reflect on the advantages and disadvantage of each one.

To make the floor plan of a room you first need to measure the space, and then write down - rather than remember - your measurements in a rough sketch. Each room should be measured separately.

Alternatively you can request your architect to provide you with the floor plan of your own house. However, you should probably need to measure your space by yourself to make sure that you have got the accurate measurements.

A 3m metal tape measure for short distances

The measuring tools you will need

Most interior spaces are quite large and you need special tools for measuring them. The most common tool is the tape measure. It gives fairly accurate measurements and it is available at very low prices in tool stores.

A fibreglass tape 20m measure with folding rewind crank for long distances. It is one of the most widely used tools by professionals. The use of this tape measure requires two people

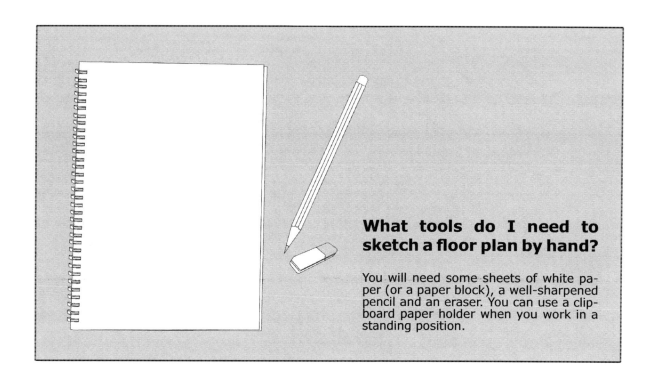

What tools do I need to sketch a floor plan by hand?

You will need some sheets of white paper (or a paper block), a well-sharpened pencil and an eraser. You can use a clipboard paper holder when you work in a standing position.

Laser distance measuring devices

If you are a professional interior designer or intend to deal professionally with arranging furniture, maybe you should consider buying a laser distance measuring device. For precise measurements the user of the device simply points with the laser beam. The device measures in inches, feet and inches, decimal feet and metric units; it gives higher accuracy when measuring than a tape measure and it can be handled by one operator.

Let's get started: How to Measure a room

For each room of your house, you must make a separate sketch and a separate furniture plan. In the following pages you will find a step-by-step guide on how to measure a room. As an example, we opted for a small room with perpendicular walls, an entrance door and a balcony door. The particular space could be the master bedroom, the children's room or your office.

Step 1: Sketch your own floor plan

The room is connected with the rest of the house through an interior door and a balcony door leads to a terrace. Once the centre of your interest is the room, there is no need to sketch the rest of the house or the terrace. Start by looking around the room. Observe carefully the proportions of the room and its shape. It is easier to capture the space, if you imagine it without furniture. The next step is to draw a free hand sketch of the floor plan on a piece of paper. Try to keep the room's proportions the way you see them. For example, observe which side is the longest and draw it relatively longer on the paper.

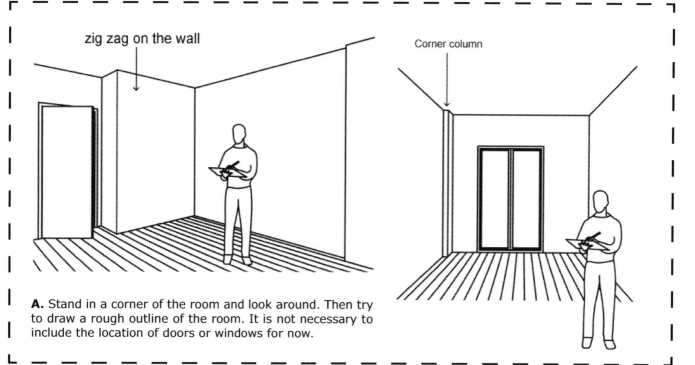

zig zag on the wall

Corner column

A. Stand in a corner of the room and look around. Then try to draw a rough outline of the room. It is not necessary to include the location of doors or windows for now.

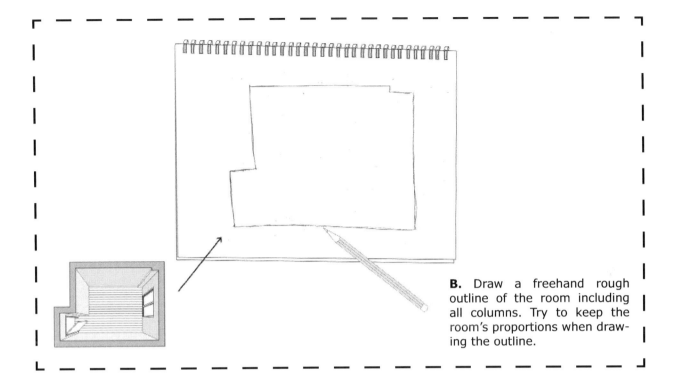

B. Draw a freehand rough outline of the room including all columns. Try to keep the room's proportions when drawing the outline.

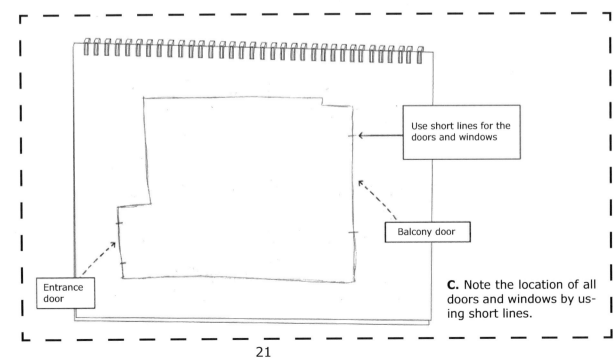

Use short lines for the doors and windows

Balcony door

Entrance door

C. Note the location of all doors and windows by using short lines.

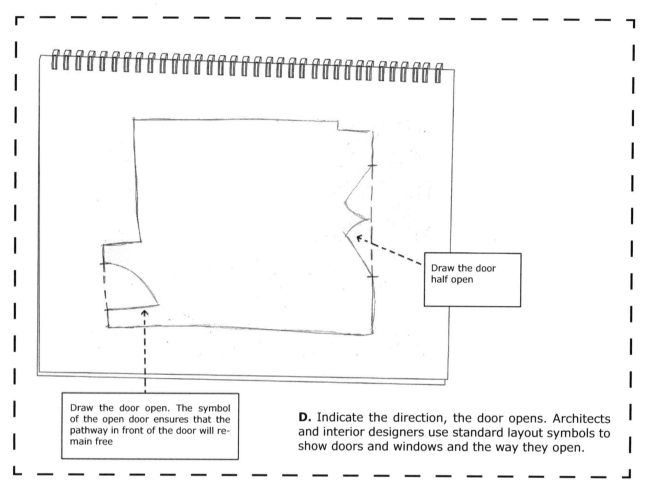

Draw the door
half open

Draw the door open. The symbol of the open door ensures that the pathway in front of the door will remain free

D. Indicate the direction, the door opens. Architects and interior designers use standard layout symbols to show doors and windows and the way they open.

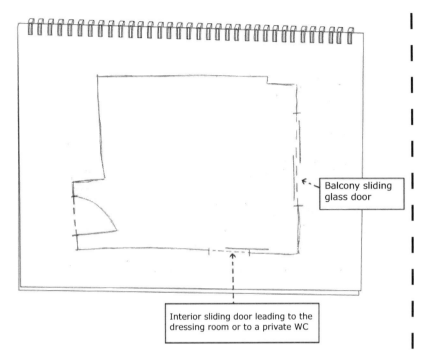

Balcony sliding glass door

Interior sliding door leading to the dressing room or to a private WC

E. Add all kind of doors and windows using appropriate symbols to your sketch. Your room may have more than one interior door and the glass door to the balcony may be sliding. There may also be a built-in closet or window in the room.

It is important to measure and note the placement of all these elements, as they affect the layout of your furniture. For example, the closet hinged doors need more free space to swing open than sliding doors.

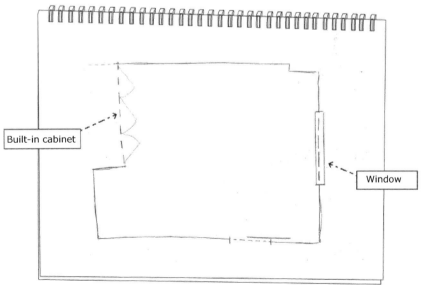

Built-in cabinet

Window

Step 2: Measure the dimensions of the room

A. Measure the overall length and width of the room with the tape measure. Try to keep the tape measure level, stretched and parallel to the wall you are measuring.

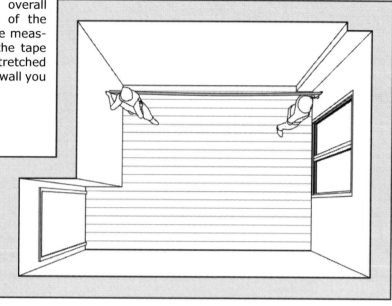

B. After every measurement you should record each dimension on your sketch in pencil, either in imperial or in metric units. If you are using metric system, dimension precision should be at two decimal places.

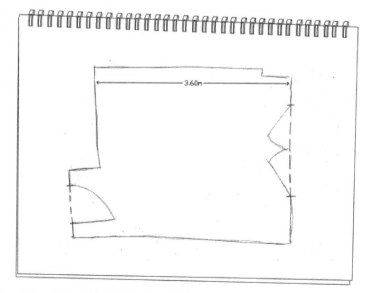

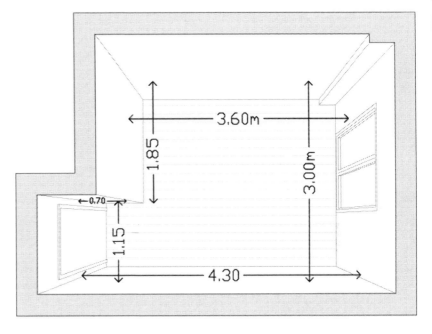

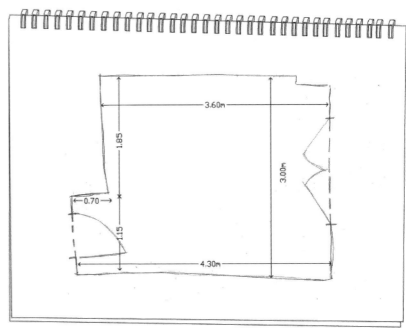

C. Continue measuring clockwise around the room until all walls are measured and all required dimensions are recorded.

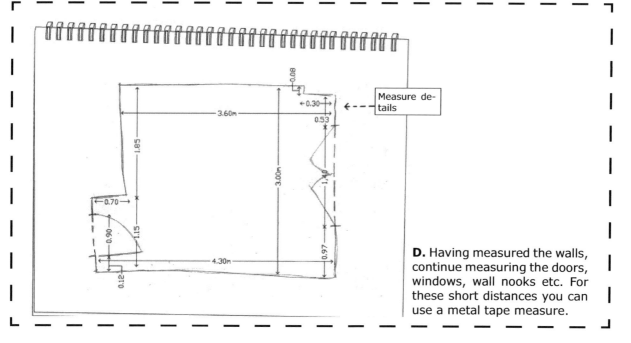

Measure details

D. Having measured the walls, continue measuring the doors, windows, wall nooks etc. For these short distances you can use a metal tape measure.

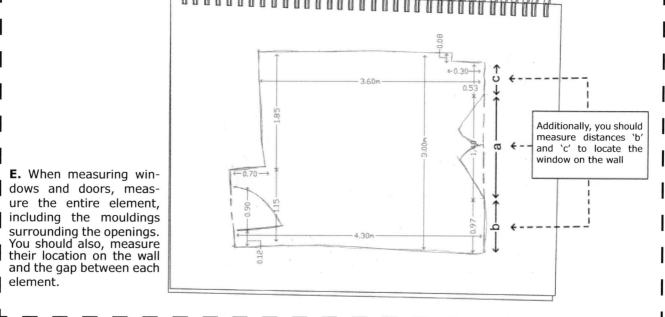

E. When measuring windows and doors, measure the entire element, including the mouldings surrounding the openings. You should also, measure their location on the wall and the gap between each element.

Additionally, you should measure distances 'b' and 'c' to locate the window on the wall

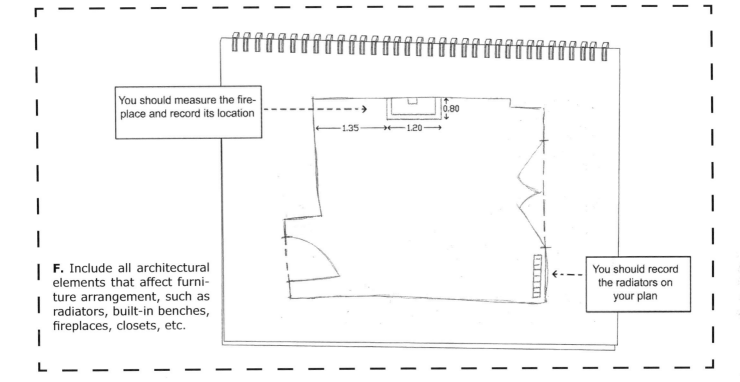

You should measure the fire-place and record its location

0.80

1.35   1.20

F. Include all architectural elements that affect furniture arrangement, such as radiators, built-in benches, fireplaces, closets, etc.

You should record the radiators on your plan

Tip: You can record the measurements on more than one floor plan sketches

Your sketch will gradually include many recorded measurements. If you like it to remain readable you may copy the sketch on a new sheet of paper and record the short dimensions and the measurements of details there.

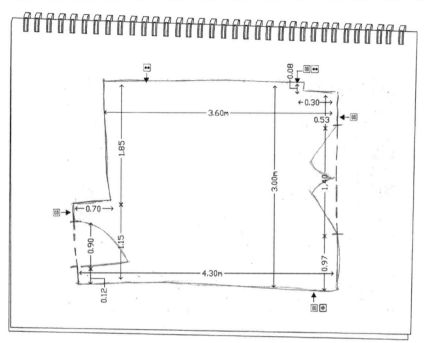

G. Optionally, record the location of electrical switches and sockets, TV antenna sockets, especially if they affect the furniture placement. For example, TV set location depends on the position of the existing TV aerial socket.

Use the center of each switch or socket as your measuring point. We must see where the wall plugs are and to avoid covering them with any furniture.

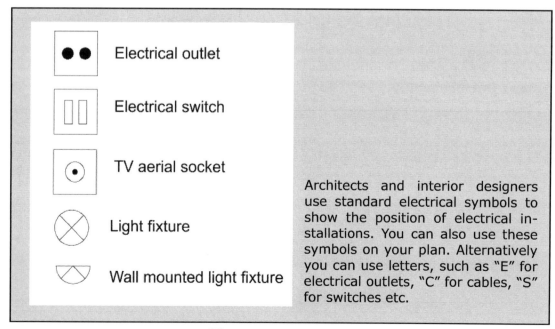

● ●	Electrical outlet
▯▯	Electrical switch
⊙	TV aerial socket
⊗	Light fixture
◖	Wall mounted light fixture

Architects and interior designers use standard electrical symbols to show the position of electrical installations. You can also use these symbols on your plan. Alternatively you can use letters, such as "E" for electrical outlets, "C" for cables, "S" for switches etc.

Step 3: Measure the existing pieces of furniture

If you are planning to use some or all pieces of your existing furniture in the new arrangement, it is necessary to measure their overall dimensions, especially the large ones. Make a list in a separate piece of paper with all furniture floor plan icons and write down the measurements. Record the quantity of furniture pieces as well.

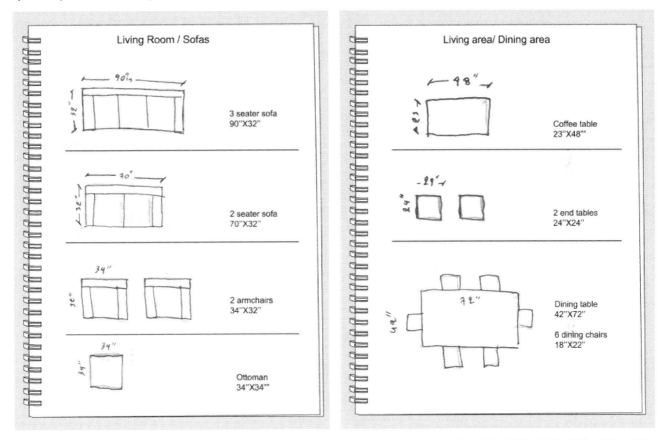

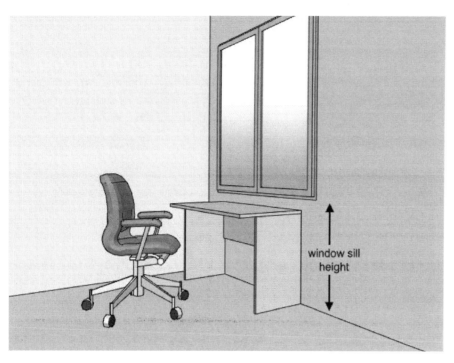

window sill
height

Do you need to measure any heights?

In some cases you will need to measure the height of specific elements. For example, you might need to measure the height of the window sill in case you want to place a study table in front of a window. The window sill must be higher that the table. You might also need to measure the overall height of the room, in case you want to place a built-in bookcase.

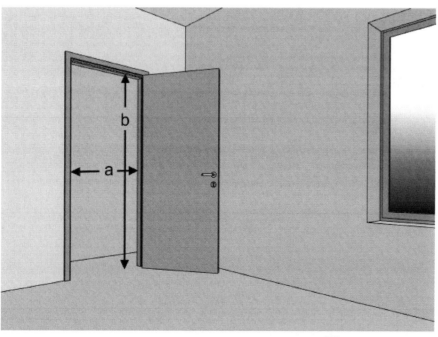

b

a

How can I be sure that large pieces will fit through doors?

Before buying new furniture, you should measure the heights and widths of any hallways, door accesses, staircases and elevators as well as the clearance of the entry. Make sure that larger pieces will fit through doors and that there is enough space for a sofa to turn in corners.

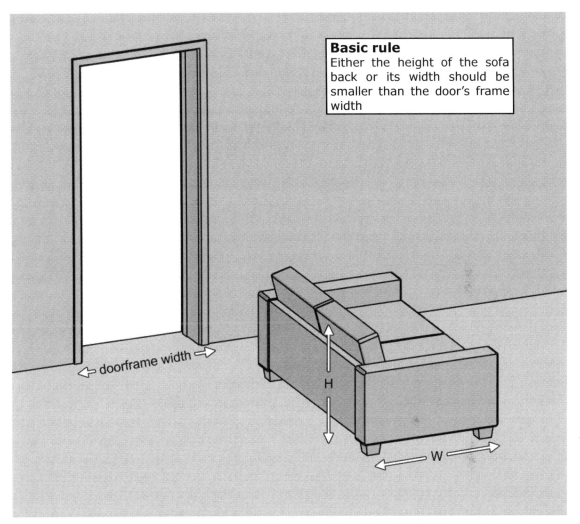

Basic rule
Either the height of the sofa back or its width should be smaller than the door's frame width

doorframe width

H

W

Purchasing a new sofa: How can I be sure that it will fit through the doorways?

The basic rule is that the height of the back of the sofa (floor to top) or the depth of its bottom (front to back) cannot exceed the minimum width of any door frame. However, if the sofa has legs with adjustable height, they may be lowered to the minimum. You can also opt for a sofa that can be brought up dismantled and then assembled in your home. Most sectional pieces can be turned upright and gently rotated through tight doorways.

2. DRAWING THE FLOOR PLAN

2. Drawing the floor plan

In order to experiment with different furniture layouts and see how a particular arrangement works you will need a floor plan at scale. Simple floor plans can be drawn by hand using a pencil and a ruler on graph paper. They can also be drawn by computer using free online design software.

If you draw the floor plan by hand you will need scaled cutouts of the furniture. A collection of cutouts is included in the Appendix I at the end of the book. You can photocopy the pages without re sizing the drawings, cut them and experiment directly on your floor plan.

In this chapter you will learn:

-How to create a simple floor plan of a room to scale
-How to use the graph paper
-How to make furniture cutouts to scale

What drawing tools and materials you will need

Pencils: Graphite drawing pencils are the main drawing tools when drafting; there are three kinds of pencils: wood–cased pencils, clutch pencils and mechanical pencils.

Sharpener: Conventional metal or polystyrene single-hole sharpeners are suitable for wood-cased pencils.

Ruler: In the imperial and U.S system a standard ruler is 12 inches or one foot long and in metric system it is 30cm long. Many rulers have metric measurements on one side and imperial measurements on the other.

Eraser: You will need a soft eraser to remove the graphite from the paper's surface in order to fix any mistakes.

Graph paper:
At the end of the book at the Appendix II, you can find sheets of 1/4" and 5mm graph paper to draw the floor plan and furniture. Alternatively you can find free kinds of graph paper online to print from your computer.

Scissors: You will need these to cut out the scale drawings of your furniture.

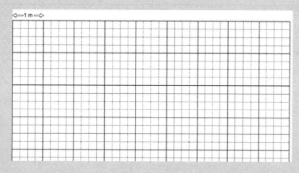

A pair of compasses: You will use it in certain occasions, i.e. if you need to draw a crooked room.

Draw at a scale using the graph paper

Floor plans should be drafted to scale, which means that the size of a room in real life should be reduced when it is drawn on a piece of paper. In the imperial and U.S system a commonly used scale for hand-drawn plans is 1/4"=1.0', which means if something is 1 foot long in real life it should be drawn 1/4 inch long. In the metric system a very common scale is 1:50, which means every 1m in real world is represented by 2cm.

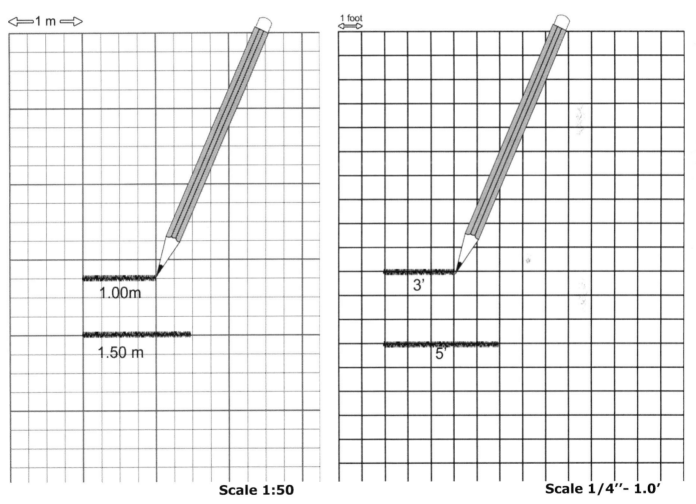

Scale 1:50   **Scale 1/4''- 1.0'**

In the metric system you can use 5mm engineering graph paper, where four boxes equal 1m of actual size

In the imperial and U.S system you can use 1/4" engineering graph paper, where one box equals a foot of actual size

Convert the sketch of the room to an architectural floor plan

A. Having the sketch of the room you have made following the instructions in the previous chapter, you can record the number of squares of graph paper you will need for each measurement.

B. Photocopy the sheet of graph paper found at the end of the book (Appendix II) according to the system of measurements you are using. You will also need a sharp#2 – HB pencil and a ruler.

C. On the graph paper select a point to start drawing. Remember to leave enough graph squares of margin around, depending on the size of your drawing. Using the pencil draw a dot on the left corner of the graph paper having left some squares of margin at each side. Using the pencil and the ruler as a straightedge, start at the dot you have made to draw a line counting the squares which represent one of the walls of your room.

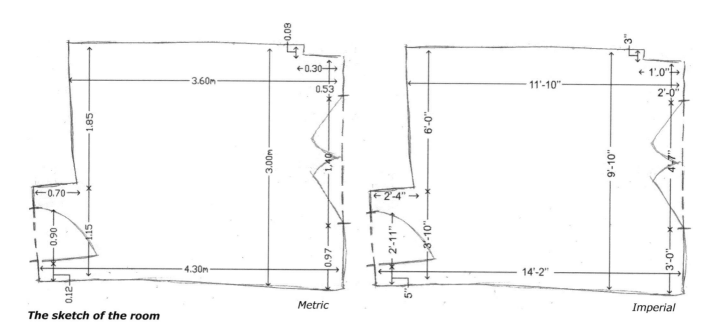

The sketch of the room

Metric

Imperial

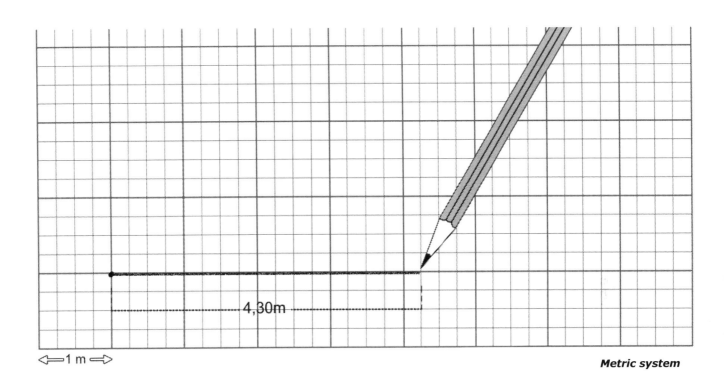

4,30m

⟸1 m ⟹

Metric system

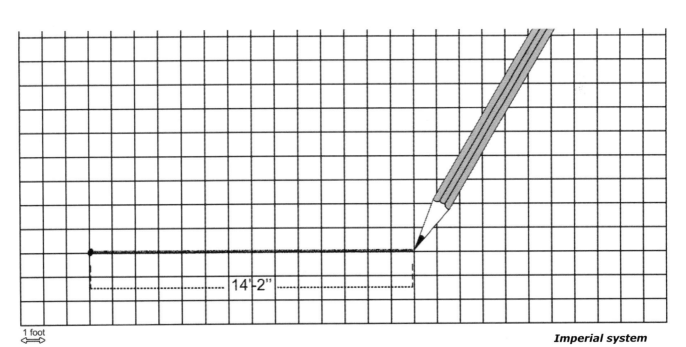

14'-2"

1 foot

Imperial system

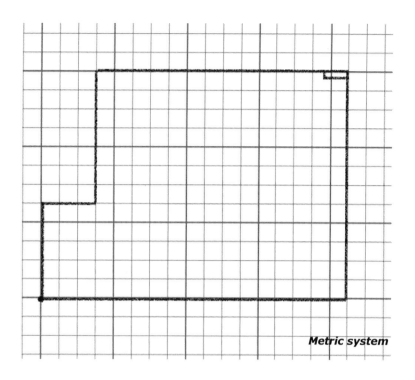

Metric system

D. Repeat the process to draw the perpendicular wall starting from the end of the first wall and continue to draw the other walls. Thus, you will create a polygon which represents the outline of the room, assuming of course that the room has parallel walls.

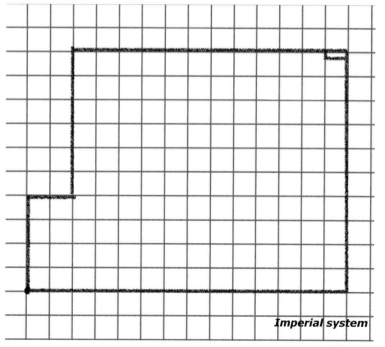

Imperial system

Note: It is possible to meet some decimals, for example if your wall is 268 inches long (22'-4"), you will need 268/12=22.33 squares to represent the length of your wall. Accordingly, if your wall measures 6.40m, you will need to multiply by 4, which means your wall will be 25.60 squares long.

In such cases you can round up or down to 22.50 and 25.50 squares referring to the previous examples. Rounding off to the nearest decimal is considered acceptable in this occasion.

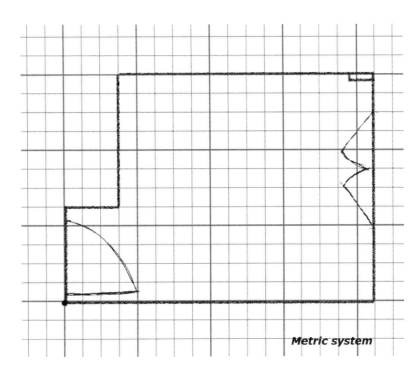

Metric system

E. Incorporate the doors and windows on the walls. Draw each window as two parallel lines and each swing door as a line with an arc. Draw each sliding door with two lines showing which panel slides. Before you draw each element you should have scaled its size and the distance showing its position on the wall and the gap between windows as well.

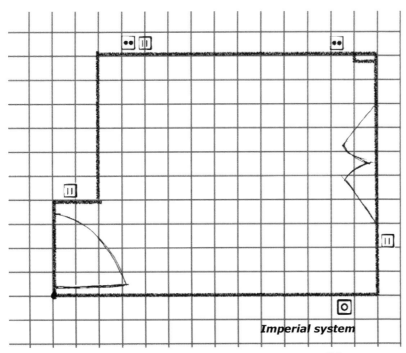

Imperial system

39

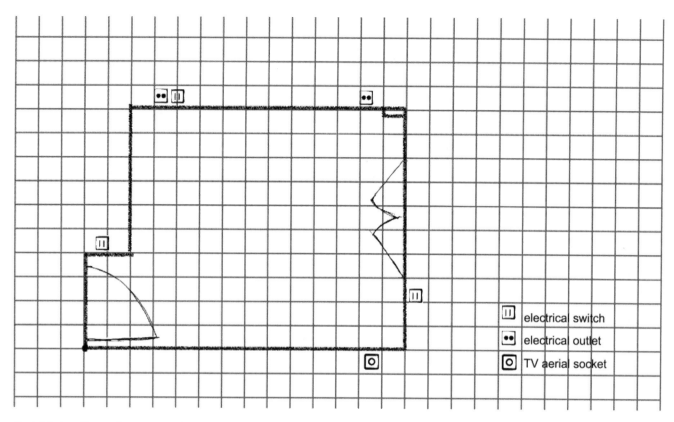

F. Add details to the room. If you have recorded the location of electrical switches, sockets and TV antenna sockets you can add these to your drawing using the relevant symbols.

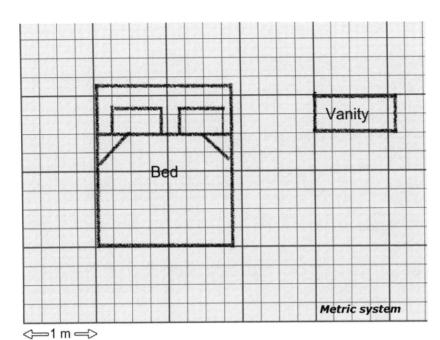

⟸1 m⟹

Experiment with the furniture cutouts

G. Draw the outline of your furniture pieces using a pencil and the ruler on the graph paper. Add a label to each piece you draw to remember later which piece of furniture it represents. You can also draw some details inside the outline of each piece, i.e. the sides and the cushions of the sofas.

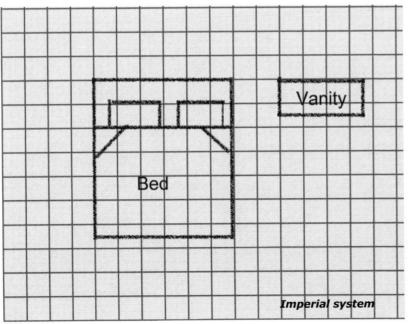

Imperial system

1 foot
⟸⟹

Tip: You can photocopy the sheet of graph paper at the end of the book on a gray sheet of paper and draw the furniture symbols onto the gray paper, so that all pieces will show up when placed on the floor plan.

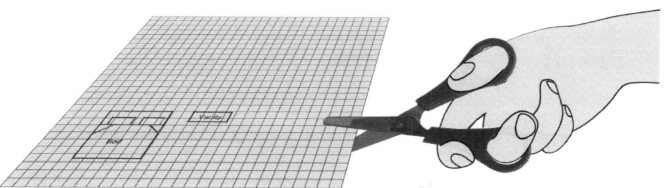

H. Make furniture cutouts using the scissors. Cut out each piece of furniture carefully.

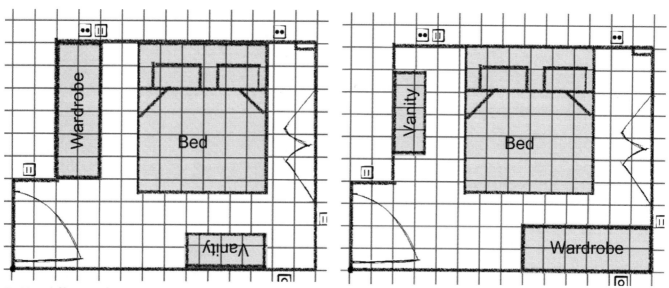

I. Try different furniture arrangements. Move around furniture cutouts to try various arrangements on the scale floor plan until you find the most suitable one.

Note: You will find a collection of furniture cutouts in scale with their measurements in the Appendix I at the end of the book. You can photocopy the pages you need, cut the furniture symbols and use the cutouts to experiment with different furniture arrangements.

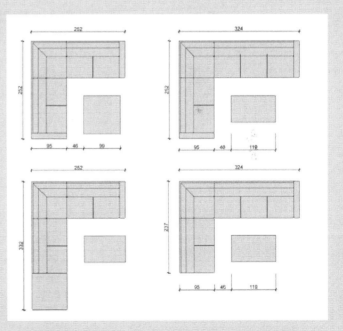

In the Appendix I at the end of the book, you'll find furniture cutouts both in metric and imperial units

3. ANALYSING SPACE

3. Analysing Space

Before experimenting with various furniture placements in any room, it is necessary to understand the space you have available. In general the spatial analysis includes

A) Room measurements

The process of measuring and writing down the measurements of the room on the floor plan sketch has been discussed in Chapter A.

B) Drafting the floor plan in scale

The floor plan design process has been discussed in Chapter B.

C) Reflecting on the characteristics of the space and your needs

At this stage you should look carefully at the room and identify all those spatial characteristics that might affect furniture arrangement, such as circulation paths, doorways, focal points, etc. On the other hand you should reflect on your needs, activities, lifestyle, etc to determine the functions of the room.

In this chapter you will learn:

- To define the circulation paths
- To identify the focal points
- To map functional zones that correspond to your activities
- To use the proportion of a room, even a disadvantageous proportion, to make a successful arrangement

Defining the needs for circulation paths

Household members walk from one room to another. Circulation is the route that people in the house follow to move from one point or area to another, such as from main entrance to the bedrooms, from a bedroom to the bathroom, from the dining room to the kitchen, etc.

Circulation in a house differs. There are paths with heavy and frequent circulation and others with secondary circulation. For example, between the main entrance of the house and the inner rooms, there is frequent circulation and the routes should be large enough without obstacles and easily accessible. On the other hand, between the main entrance and the balcony doors the circulation is low, so the paths could be more playful, longer, turning, etc.

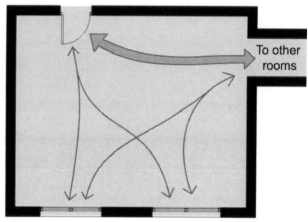

The main entrance of the house is through the living room and the rest of the rooms are being accessed through an opening on the right wall. Consequently, a heavy circulation route is created between the main entrance and the opening. On the other hand, the balcony doors are not accessed daily, especially during the winter months.

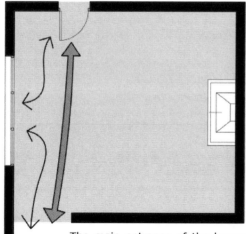

The main entrance of the house is through the living room and the rest of the rooms are being accessed through an opening on the opposite wall. The terrace or the courtyard is also accessed via the same route. Consequently, one circulation path is enough to connect the entrance with the rooms and the courtyard, while enough space is kept for arranging the living room.

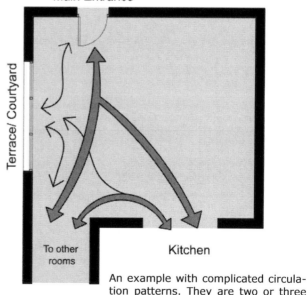

An example with complicated circulation patterns. They are two or three main circulation paths and several secondary ones.

Circulation paths / measurements

The width of the circulation path depends on the frequency of the circulation and the traffic load. In general, we must consider two types of paths: the main circulation paths with heavy and frequent traffic and the secondary with low and rare traffic. Though apart from the paths, sometimes we must ensure circulation between some pieces of furniture in order to reach and use them, to clean the in-between space, etc.

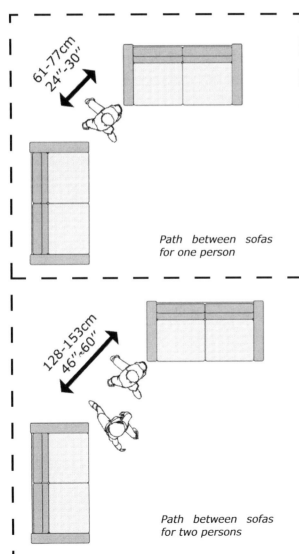

61-77cm
24"-30"

*Path between sofas
for one person*

128-153cm
46"-60"

*Path between sofas
for two persons*

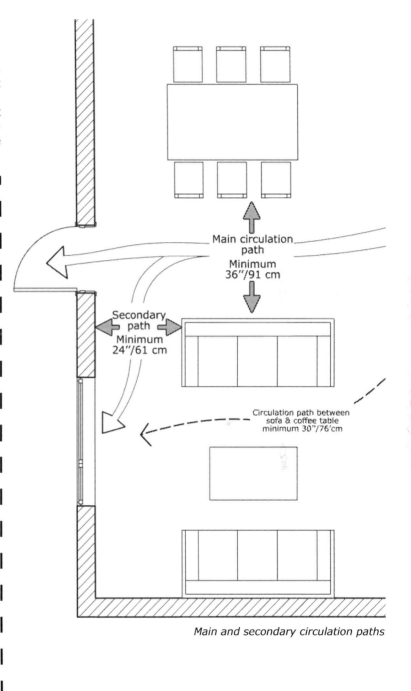

Main circulation
path
Minimum
36"/91 cm

Secondary
path
Minimum
24"/61 cm

Circulation path between
sofa & coffee table
minimum 30"/76 cm

Main and secondary circulation paths

47

Finding the focal points

The issue of focal points concerns primarily the arrangement of the living room. As focal points can be defined the fireplace, a great view, the piano, an artwork or the TV. The room's focal point will usually dictate the direction and orientation of the seating in the living room.

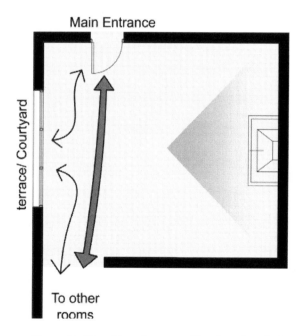

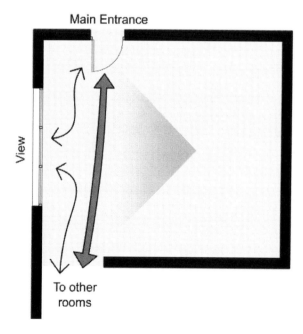

Case A: The fireplace as the focal point
The fireplace on the right draws our attention to the right wall. This might imply that the sofa should be placed towards the fireplace.

Case B: The view as the focal point
If, however, there was no fireplace but a great view through the window, it might imply that the sofa should be dragged towards the window.

Mapping the functional zones

A room does not serve the same purpose for all inhabitants. Take for example the living room. For some users, this room should be formal, closed to daily activities, clean and tidy, to be entered only when guests come. For others, the living room is a casual space for everyday life, where family members gather daily, discuss, have meals, watch television, etc. Thus, there are more than one solutions for each space, which depend on our needs, our habits, our preferences, etc.

In a living room for example, there may be the following functions
- Socializing (formal living room)
- Gossiping with family members (sitting area)
- Recreation
- Watching television and movies
- Listening to music
- Reading books/newspapers
- Doing Paperwork
- Working with computer/surfing the internet

If space allows, the living room could be divided into two zones: for example in one corner could be created a formal living room and in the other an informal sitting area for watching TV. For some users, it is necessary to include in the living room an area for paperwork or hobbies, placing for example a desk, a bookcase, some shelves, etc. After reflecting on your needs, activities and on the functional zones you want to fit in a room, you should start thinking a way of arranging furniture in order to perform these activities.

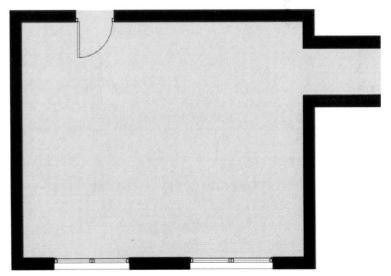

Consider the particular space. Lets suppose that you want to fit in this space both the living area and the dining area. What option do you have? How would you arrange the functional zones?

49

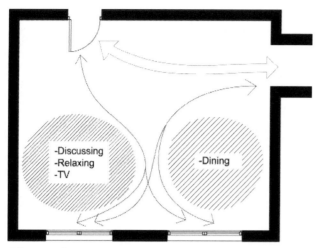

Alternative A: *Two functional areas can be developed: a living (discussing, relaxing, watching TV) area and a dining one.*

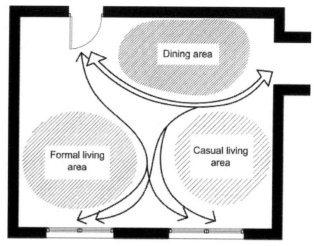

Alternative B: *Three functional areas can be created: a formal sitting area, a casual sitting area and a dinning one. The most obvious disadvantage of the dining area is the small space, so a sideboard may not fit. Another drawback is that the dining area might block the circulation path.*

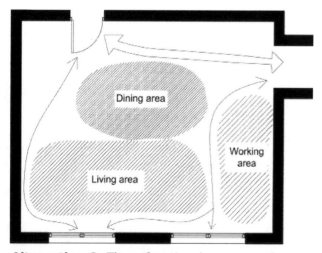

Alternative C: *Three functional areas can be created: a living area, a dining area and a working one.*

> **Note:** None of the initial layouts should be excluded in case you would like to review them later. Besides, in this step you are just investigating your own space dynamics.

Analyse the proportion of space

The proportion of an interior space is qualified by the relative length of three variables: width, length, and height. Furniture arrangement is strongly influenced by the proportion of space. A room that is relatively long and narrow is much different than a square room. The relative proportion of a room determines whether a space can be used as a path or a place. In general, square rooms are difficult to furnish while rectangular spaces are easier, since functional zones can be placed along a main circulation path.

Take for example the following rooms which are the same size but different in proportion.
- Open large square spaces can be divided into smaller areas by grouping furniture.
- A rectangular space can be broken down into different zones to accommodate distinct needs. Say, half of the space is for the sofa, serving the function of conversing and the other half is for a dining set, serving the function of dining.

Living rooms which are the same size but different in proportion

Square living room

A square living room is one of the most difficult rooms to arrange. Here, an additional challenge arises: the square living room has three entrances, which limit experimenting with various furniture placements. Defining the television as the focal point allows you to arrange furniture centered around it. L-shaped asymmetrical arrangement around the coffee table allows a circulation path to the patio door. Another circulation path is left from one entrance to the other. The square shape of the room allows only one function, which is socializing.

Rectangular living room

A rectangle is the most common shape for a room. In a large rectangular room you may arrange a living/dining room combo, meaning two activities. Here, an additional challenge arises: the rectangular room is relatively narrow. You can place two loveseats facing each other parallel to the narrow walls. Loveseats are shorter than sofas and provide comfortable conversation areas. They also allow pathways between the long wall and the end of the sofas, leading from one entrance to the other. Moreover, you can position a wall-mounted TV on the longer wall opposite the sitting area. Finally, you can situate a dining set to break the rectangular space into two distinct open plan spaces.

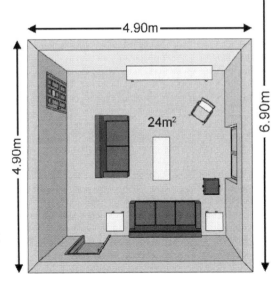

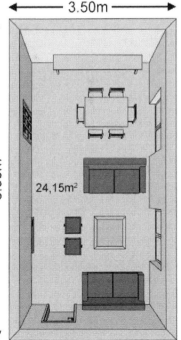

4.   LIVING   AREA

4. Living area

The living/sitting room is the room where we spend time with our family, welcome visitors, relax, chat, watch television, read a good book, etc. In larger houses, the living room may be used for more formal and quiet gatherings, while a separate room, such as a family room or a recreation room is used for leisure and informal ones. The living room needs to be inviting and comfortable. Regardless of its size, it is one of the most visible and important areas of our home.

The typical Western living room contains furnishings, such as sofas, chairs, occasional tables, bookshelves, floor lamps or other furniture. The possibilities of various living room layouts are almost endless and there are many alternative ways to arrange and group furniture pieces. A conversation area for example, can be created either by grouping a sofa, two armchairs and a coffee table or by selecting a sectional instead. Furniture can be also used to separate functional areas. For example, by floating a sofa in the middle of the living room we can divide the dining from the living area within an open plan.

In this chapter you will learn:

- The types of living room furniture and their standard measurements
- Clearances, optimum distances, allowances, circulation path widths, etc.
- Types of living room layouts and seating area arrangements

- Guidelines for different TV placements

Types of seating furniture

Sofas generally serve purposes such as relaxing, taking a nap, reading a book, chatting with friends and family, taking drinks, etc. Considerations about sofas are mostly personal, affecting both the sofa purchase and its placement in the space. For example, if the family members gather frequently in the living room, a large sectional sofa seems an appropriate and cosy solution for them. If users take a nap on the sofa in front of the TV, a suitable solution could be two long sofas arranged either in L-shape or in face-to-face arrangement. If users need a quiet and relaxing corner in the room for reading and listening to music, an armchair with an ottoman, a side table and a floor lamp could be ideal to serve this purpose. If there are kids in the house, large cushions spread on the floor are necessary accessories in the living room. It all depends on the users' needs and lifestyle.

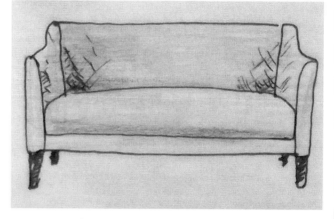

Loveseats

Loveseats are one of the most popular couch types. A loveseat is a small sofa designed for a maximum of two people to sit comfortably.

Sofas

Manufacturers usually produce sofas in various lengths. There are usually 2-seater and 3-seater sofas. Moreover, you can also find 2,5-seater and extra large 3-seater sofas.

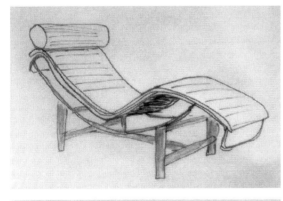

Chaise longue

A chaise longue (which is literally translated in English as "long chair") is a sofa in the shape of a chair that is long enough to support the legs. Sometimes any long reclining chair is referred as a chaise longue.

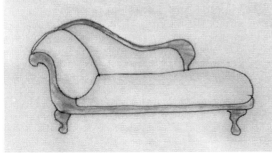

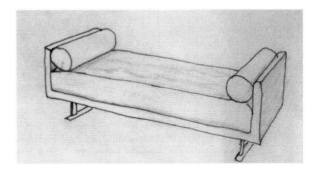

Sofa beds

A sofa bed, also called a sleeper sofa, is a sofa with a built-in bed. The sofa transforms into a bed through a mechanism which allows the bed part to fold into the sofa base when not needed. This piece of furniture is a great alternative for a guest room, as it accommodates overnight guests.

Whether you're purchasing a sofa bed for the bed part or the couch part, you should keep under consideration that it will be used as a sofa more frequently. This means that the important factors are its size, style and comfort as a sofa and not as a bed.

Futons

Futon is originated from Japanese beds which consist of a cotton filled mattress that can be folded when not in use. Its definition has developed into a chair or a couch with a flimsier frame than a normal one that can be transformed into some sort of bed.

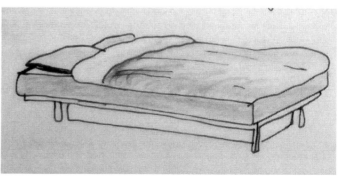

Bean bags (also beanbags)

It is a sack made out of durable fabric or leather filled with dried beans, urethane, expanded polystyrene or expanded polypropylene. It is directly placed on the floor and serves as an alternative to a chair.

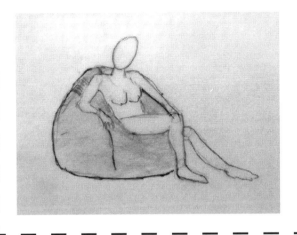

Ottomans

An ottoman, also known as a footstool or pouf, is an upholstered seat without a back or arms often used as a footstool and occasionally as a coffee table. Ottomans usually accompany armchairs or gliders. In some cases they are hollow and serve as storage units and in others long and leather and they serve as sofas. There are many variations used in the bedroom, the family room or the guest room.

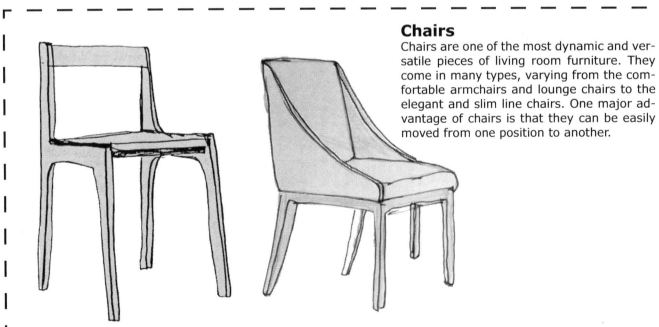

Chairs

Chairs are one of the most dynamic and versatile pieces of living room furniture. They come in many types, varying from the comfortable armchairs and lounge chairs to the elegant and slim line chairs. One major advantage of chairs is that they can be easily moved from one position to another.

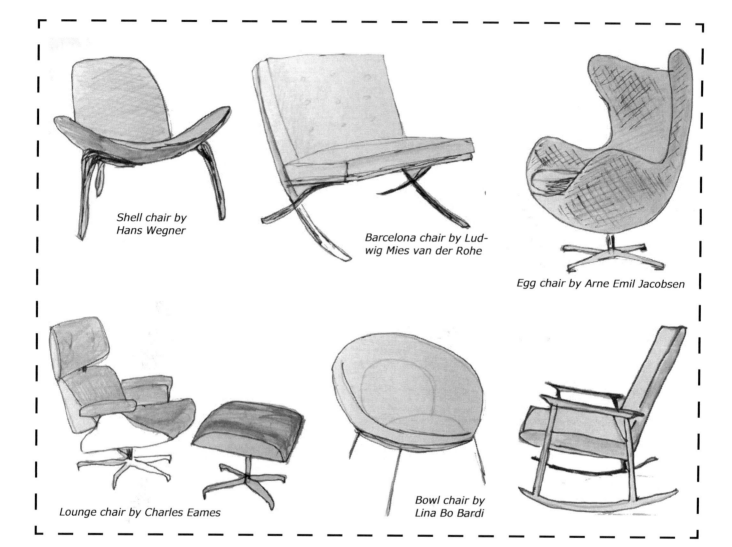

Shell chair by
Hans Wegner

Barcelona chair by Lud-
wig Mies van der Rohe

Egg chair by Arne Emil Jacobsen

Lounge chair by Charles Eames

Bowl chair by
Lina Bo Bardi

Sectional Sofas

A sectional sofa, usually called "sectional", is composed of several units (usually two, three or four) and includes at least two pieces at an angle measuring 90 degrees or greater. This modular system offers flexible and comfortable seating, comes in a variety of units, from chairs to loveseats, ottomans, and chaises that can easily be combined to meet your needs. L-shaped sectionals can define spaces; for example, positioning the back of a sectional to face the dining area defines a living-room grouping in a great room or a house with an open floor plan.

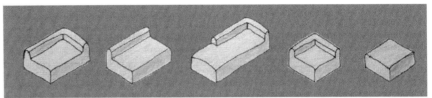

Units of a sectional sofa

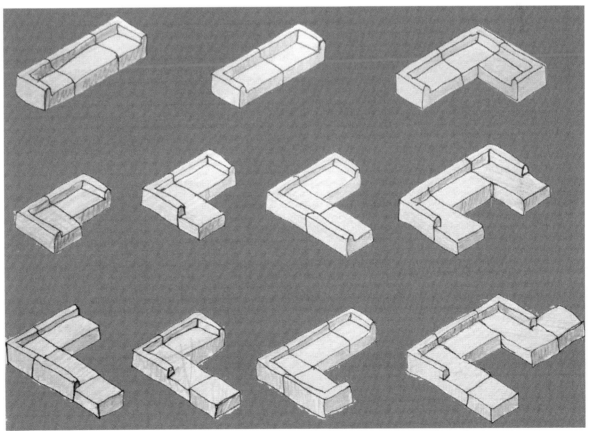

Different sectional arrangements

Typical sofa measurements

Most furniture pieces are manufactured to standard measurements in a wide variety of styles, colors or upholstery fabrics. The majority of them have the same approximate measurements. However, before actually purchasing a sofa you need to measure it to ensure that it will fit inside the provided space.

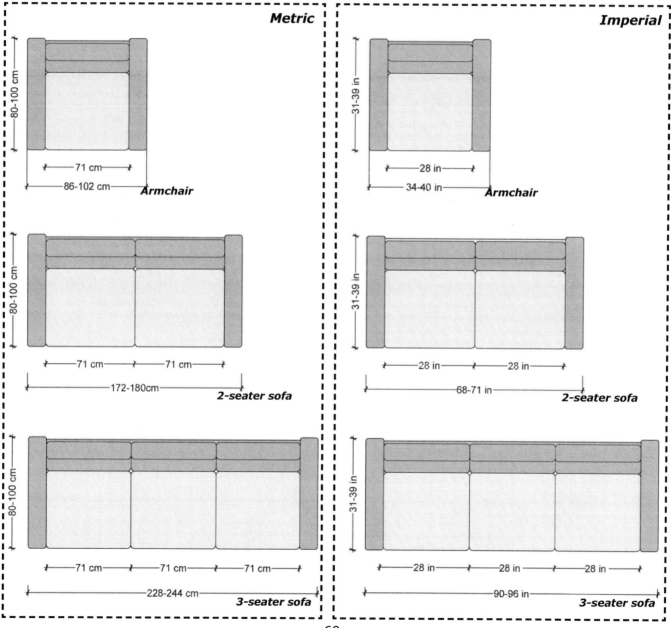

Metric

80-100 cm
71 cm
86-102 cm *Armchair*

80-100 cm
71 cm — 71 cm
172-180cm *2-seater sofa*

80-100 cm
71 cm — 71 cm — 71 cm
228-244 cm *3-seater sofa*

Imperial

31-39 in
28 in
34-40 in *Armchair*

31-39 in
28 in — 28 in
68-71 in *2-seater sofa*

31-39 in
28 in — 28 in — 28 in
90-96 in *3-seater sofa*

Notice: There are exceptions to the measurements

You should always keep in mind that there are always exceptions to sofa measurements. So, if you are planning on purchasing new furniture pieces you should read the given measurements or measure them by yourself. If you are planning to use existing pieces you should also measure them using the tape to ensure that they will fit in your new layout.

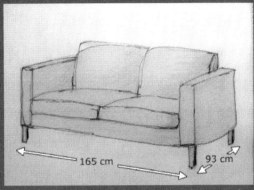

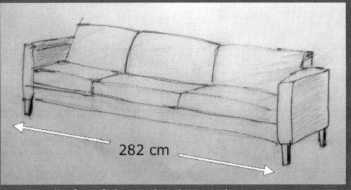

An example of a sofa shorter than the typical range

An example of a sofa longer that the typical range

Coffee table measurements

A coffee table, also known as a cocktail table, is positioned in front of sofas and is used to hold beverages, magazines, books and various small items you may need while sitting. Coffee tables also serve as storage units when they come with incorporated cabinets.

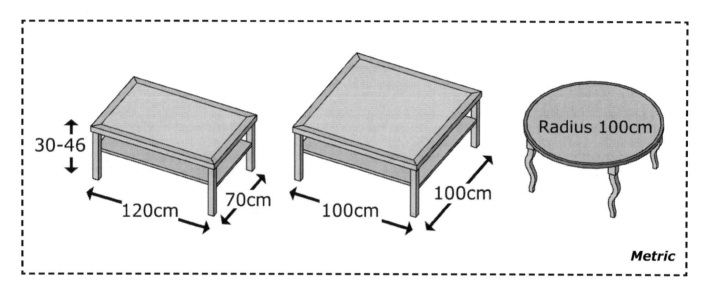

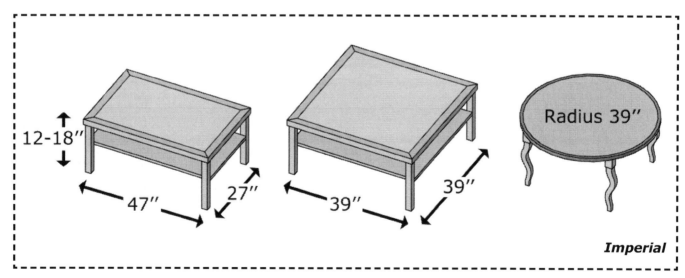

Coffee table height in relation to seat height

A coffee table is a low table having about the same height as the sofa seat or slightly lower. Thus, the coffee table becomes suitable to hold your beverages, snack plates, magazines, books or other small items you may need while seated.

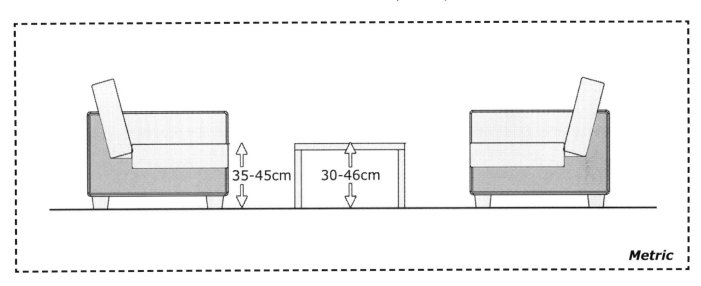

35-45cm 30-46cm

Metric

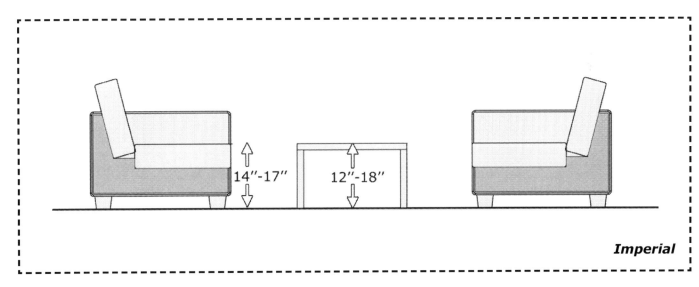

14"-17" 12"-18"

Imperial

End tables

An end table is not selected to just add an accent to a living room. It mainly provides a place on either side of a sofa to set down magazines, remote controls, drinks or food. Usually, the end tables are a few inches shorter than the sofa arms, so that they can be easily accessed from the sofa. Picture frames, table lights and other small decorative objects can be beautifully displayed on an end table. Placing a reading lamp on an end table provides focused lighting for reading on the sofa.

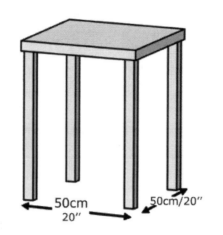

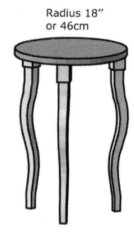

Radius 18" or 46cm

50cm 20"

50cm/20"

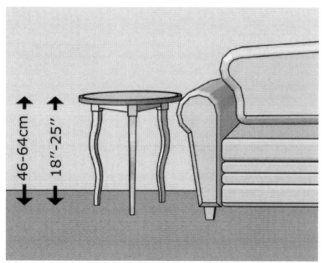

46-64cm

18"-25"

The height of an end table

The rule of thumb is that the end table surface area should be equal to or just below the height of the sofa arms. Since a standard sofa arm height is around 24-25 inches/60 to 64cm, most end tables should be between 22 and 30 inches/55 to 76cm high. However, you should always measure your sofa arm to be sure, since arm heights vary from sofa to sofa.

An end table is not supposed to be higher than a sofa arm. Having the tabletop above the sofa arm level can cause problems, such as difficulties in setting a drink on the table or picking things off of it, etc. If you can't find end tables matching your sofas within your target height range, opt for a shorter rather than a higher table. However, select end tables that are no more than 2"/5cm lower than the arm height.

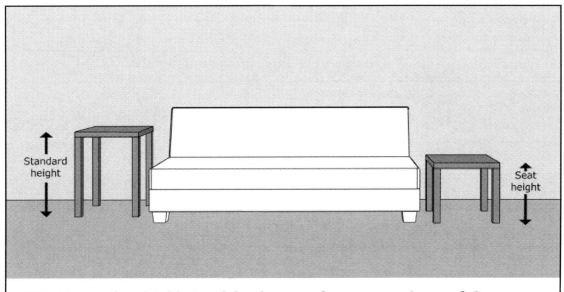

What type of end table to pick when you have an armless sofa?
If you have an armless sofa you have two options: either to select end tables with height at sofa arms would normally sit 24 to 25 inches/61 to 64 cm or purchase low models that are level with the sofa seat 14 to 17 inches/35 to 45 cm. Both options are equivalent. The selection of either option depends on your preferences and your space design.

Clearances-Distance between sofas and coffee tables

Clearance between the seat and the edge of the coffee table should allow a seated person to access the coffee table without rising. At the same time clearance should allow free foot movement and a comfortable seating and rising.

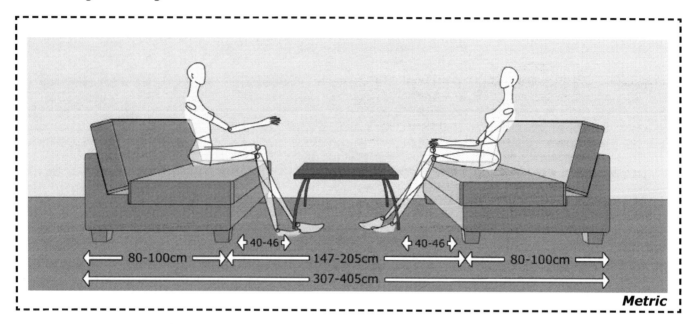

Metric

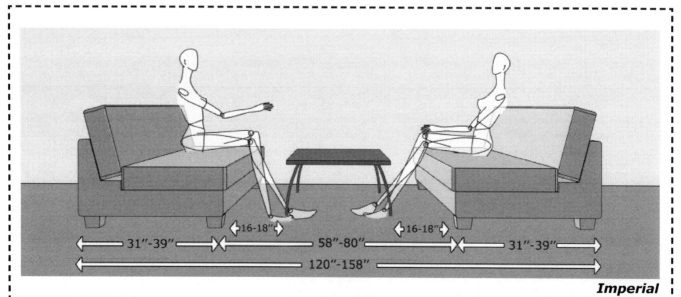

Imperial

66

Conversation distance

Two people sitting across from each other must be within a specific dimensional range for a comfortable conversation.

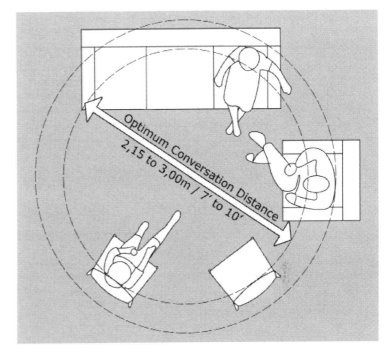

Optimal conversation distance
The optimal conversation distance is between 215 and 300cm/84" and 218"

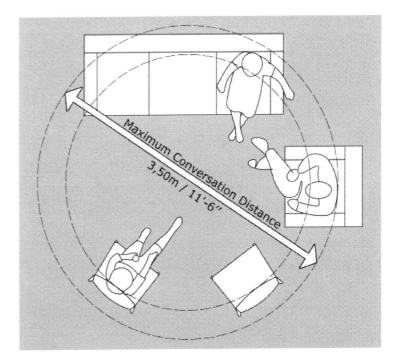

Maximum conversation distance
Maximum conversation distance between two people is approximately 350cm/138"

Space behind a sofa - Allowances

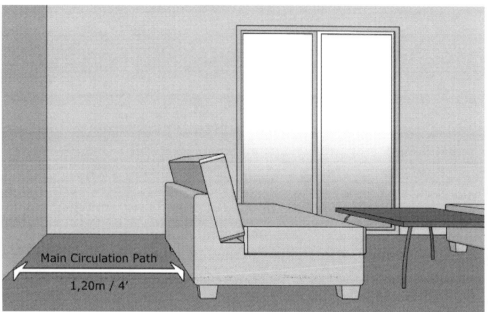

Main Circulation Path
1,20m / 4'

If the space behind a sofa serves as a main circulation path you should allow approximately 4'/120cm between the back of the sofa and the wall. Although the minimum distance for a person to pass can be smaller 2'/60cm, this narrow distance is advisable only for secondary paths.

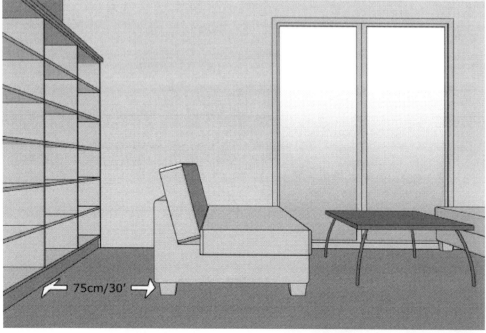

75cm/30'

If you have installed a bookcase against a wall, a minimum of 30"/75cm is required for a path between the back of the sofa and the front of the bookcase for accessing the books.

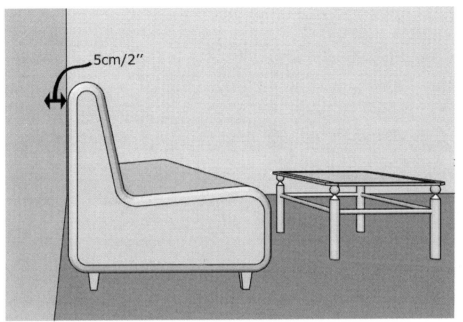

5cm/2"

Allowance between the wall and the sofa

When positioning sofas against a wall, you should allow at least one or two inches/2.50 to 5cm between the wall and the sofa. This prevents upholstery damage that can result from a sofa rubbing repeatedly against the wall. It also protects the wall from scratches and accidents caused by abrupt contacts with the sofa.

Circulation between sofas in L-shaped arrangements

When you create an L-shaped arrangement with two sofas, you can allow in-between circulation for one or two persons. However, due to this placement some people may be seated away from each other and the conversation between them may become troublesome.

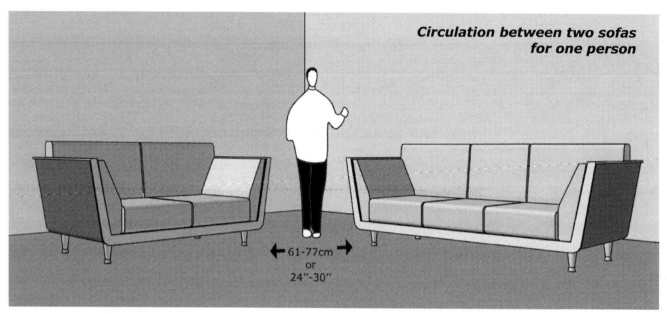

Circulation between two sofas for one person

61-77cm
or
24"-30"

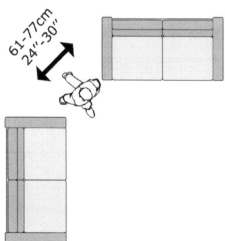

61-77cm
24"-30"

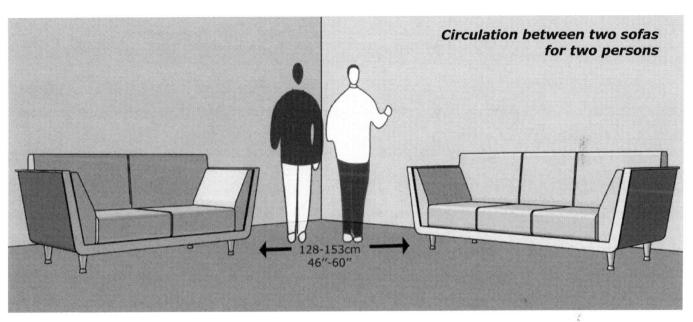

Circulation between two sofas for two persons

128-153cm
46"-60"

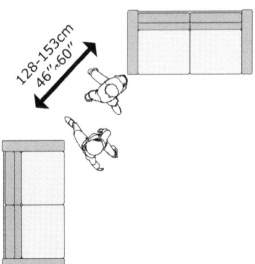

128-153cm
46"-60"

Circulation between the sofa & the coffee table

You can create a circulation area between the sofa and the coffee table allowing a large distance between the sofa and the table. In this case people will be in a difficult position to reach the coffee table while they are sitting.

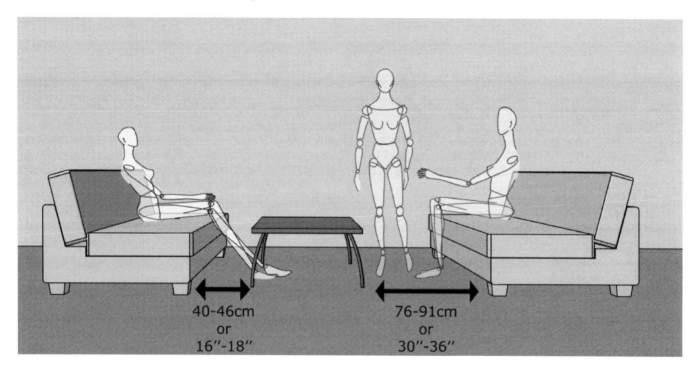

40-46cm
or
16"-18"

76-91cm
or
30"-36"

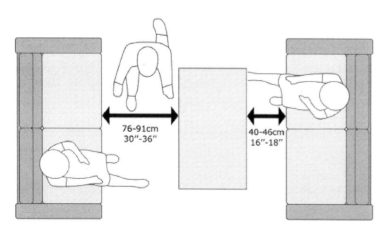

76-91cm
30"-36"

40-46cm
16"-18"

72

Living room layouts

Living room furniture arrangement should encourage conversation, be inviting and support eye contact and normal tone speech. The pieces of furniture and decorative objects should be spread evenly all over the living room, avoiding overcrowding in one side of the room.

73

SYMMETRICAL ARRANGEMENT

Balance in a space refers to the ways items in this space are arranged to create a unified whole. Two types of balance can be found: symmetrical and asymmetrical. Symmetry is the way of placing objects to produce a mirror image, such as placing two table lamps at either end of a sofa or two chairs at either end of a table.

Two identical chaise longues with a pendant lamp above them create a mirror like image. The coffee table and the fireplace on the axis amplify the sense of symmetry.

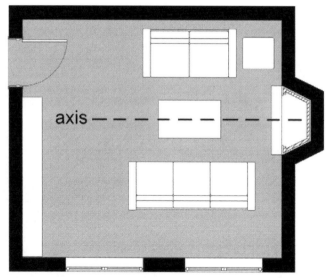

You can create a symmetrical living room layout by using the center of a room or a central architectural feature, such as the fireplace or a window. You can place the furniture symmetrically on either side of the imaginary axis passing through these elements.

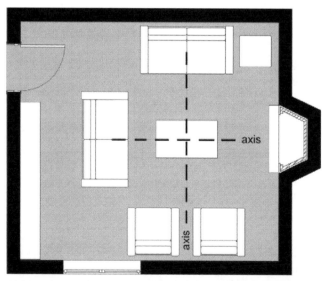

The items used in a symmetrical design should not be identical; however, they should be approximately of the same height or similar in form and shape. In the layout above, there are two axes; the two armchairs are symmetrical along one of the symmetry axes and to the loveseat opposite, along the second symmetry axis.

74

ASYMMETRICAL ARRANGEMENT

Instead of a symmetrical furniture arrangement along one or two axes, you can asymmetrically place the furniture pieces to get a fresh and casual feel. Symmetry is generally restful, creates a sense of balance in the space, while asymmetry offers visual motion and excitement. Asymmetry may also refer to an imbalance, such as placing two chairs of different sizes next to each other. Asymmetry is less obvious and requires a lot of thought.

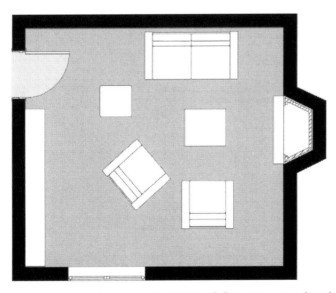

In the layout above, some pieces of furniture are placed asymmetrically and some others symmetrically. Typically, symmetry and asymmetry are working together. For example, a strictly symmetrical arrangement can be enriched by placing the accessories asymmetrically.

Notice: If you decide to use sofas of different styles instead of a pair of identical ones, make sure that the seat height is similar.

75

Right angle VS Diagonal arrangement

The most common furniture arrangement is at right angles or parallel to the walls. Rooms usually have rectangular shapes. However, in some cases you can consider placing furniture at an angle. Angled arrangement allows you to position furniture pieces away from the wall and can sometimes make a small space appear larger.

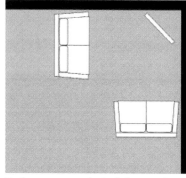 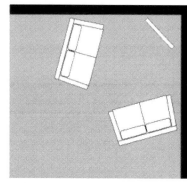

Sofas arranged at right angles   *Sofas arranged in a V shape*

The TV is placed kitty-corner. The two sofas can either be arranged at right angles or at a slant, like a V shape. This arrangement creates a cosy and informal corner, allowing everyone sitting to see each other and watch TV at the same time.

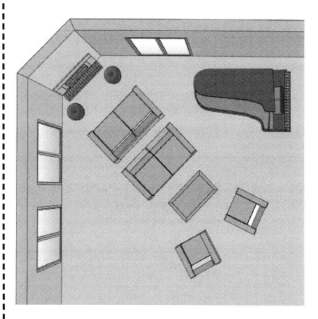

In this living room layout the fireplace is a starting point. A cosy conversation area is created parallel to fireplace. This arrangement allows comfortable circulation paths from the entrance to the balcony doors.

Large pieces VS small pieces

Smaller furniture pieces are more versatile as they can easily move and rotate; they also work well for downsizing. Larger pieces are usually more comfortable and luxurious suitable for large spaces. Large pieces of furniture, i.e. sofas, can be replaced by smaller pieces maintaining the same number of seaters. For example, a 2-seater sofa can be replaced either by two armchairs or by two dining chairs or even by two ottomans.

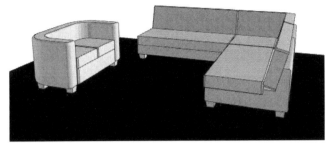

U shaped living room with a sectional sofa and a loveseat for 6 seaters minimum

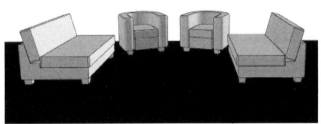

U shaped living room with two armchairs and two sofas for 6 seaters minimum

Floating Furniture into the living room

People often push larger furnishings against walls, assuming that it's the only option they've got. However, they can float furniture into a room. Groups of furniture can be used to define a space, such as the living area, the conversation area, the TV area, etc. The back of a sofa, especially a sectional sofa, can act as a divider between two spaces. If you like to try floating your furniture and you don't really know how to start, try the following trick. Place your coffee table in the center of the room and pull your sofa and chairs around the table, making sure that the arrangement doesn't block an entry, circulation path or doorway.

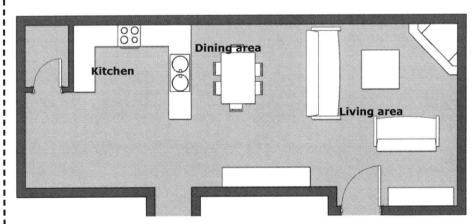

The back of the 3-seater sofa not only creates a conversation area, but also divides the dining area from the living area

The flexibility of chairs and small pieces of furniture

Chairs are the most versatile pieces of furniture in the living room. If you exclude the large heavy armchairs, normal ones take up very little space. They can be easily rearranged to meet temporary needs and extra pieces offer extra sitting space. Ottomans and puffs are also small sized light pieces that can serve the same purpose.

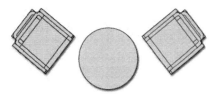

A pair of chairs with a coffee table can convert a corner or an empty spot into a private area for two

Chairs not only complement sectional sofas with extra seating space, but accompanied by an end table, they can also create a semi-independent corner for two-people

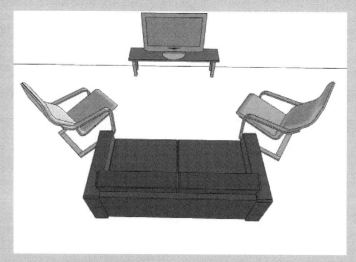

In this arrangement the two relax chairs complement the sofa. The chairs can be either used to create a conversation area or can be turned facing the TV

Seating furniture layouts

As sofa is one of the largest pieces of furniture, your primary consideration when deciding the living room layout is the sofa placement. Once
you determine the sofa position, all other furniture pieces, such as
chairs and coffee tables fall into place.

Generally, the steps in sofa arrangement process are the following
a) You decide where to place your sofa
b) You decide the position of smaller pieces, such as the loveseat and
the armchairs
c) You decide the position of occasional chairs, the coffee table, etc
d) You think of selecting accessories, such as pillows, table lamps, etc.

79

L-Shaped arrangements

L-shaped arrangements are an ideal option for small or odd-shaped spaces. You can float one or both sofas in the room or arrange them against the walls of a corner. You can also place the open part of an L-shaped arrangement facing the fireplace or a window for a scenic outdoor view.

Using a 3-seater sofa and a 2-seater sofa (or loveseat)

You can place a sofa and a loveseat in an L-shaped arrangement facing a focal point (a window, a fireplace or the TV). Tuck an end table in the space between the sofas with a table lamp on the table top to light up the area for reading, hobbies etc.

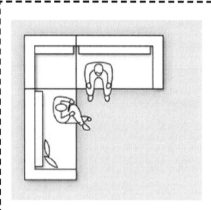

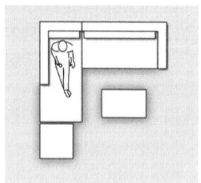

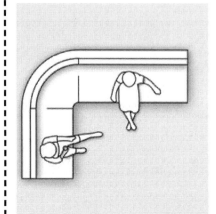

Using a Sectional Sofa

A sectional sofa with its multiple pieces can provide various seating options, offering plenty of space for a comfortable lounge. You can pick pieces that form an L-shaped sofa with/without a built-in chaise or an ottoman footrest and armed/armless end units. You can situate an end table at either side of the sectional and a coffee table to fill the empty space in front of the sofa. Occasionally, you can add ottomans and floor pillows to accommodate extra guests.

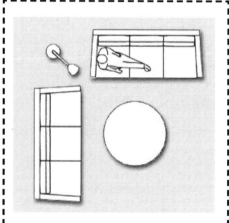

Using 3-seater sofas

You can place two sofas in an L-shaped arrangement facing a focal point (a window with a view, a fireplace or the TV). Inbetween the two sofas, you can place a floor lamp or an end table with a table lamp.

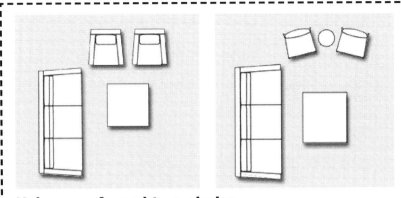

Using a sofa and two chairs
A preferable solution in case there is not enough space and there are not so many visitors.

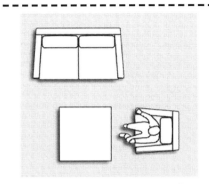

Using a loveseat and a chair
This seating arrangement is ideal for tiny apartments, and also for creating a reading/chatting nook in larger ones.

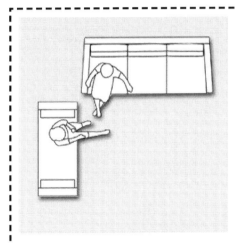

Using a sofa and a chaise longue
You can place a sofa and a chaise longue in an L-shaped arrangement to create a cosy and relaxing nook. A chaise longue is suitable for reading books, daydreaming, listening music, etc.

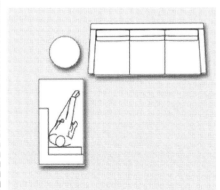

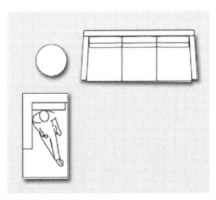

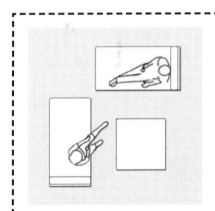

Using two chaise longues
A seating arrangement that is ideal for relaxing, reading a good book, listening to music, etc.

Face to face arrangements (Parallel arrangements)

Arranging sofas and armchairs facing each other creates an ideal conversation area. Inbetween you can place a coffee table or a large rectangular ottoman bench to supply a convenient table to place a tray of food and snacks or to serve as a foot rest. This arrangement is ideal for emphasizing a focal point, such as a fireplace or a beautiful view. The sofas are placed to face each other with the focal point centered at an open end of the sofa arrangement. Usually, the sofas look better when they float into the room, so you should avoid placing them against walls.

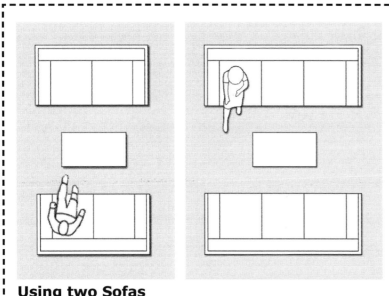

Using two Sofas
You can 2-seater or 3-seater sofas. They should not necessarily be of the same style, fabric, color or measurements.

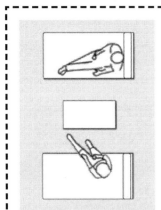

Using two chaise longues
An arrangement ideal for relaxing, reading books, listening to music, meditating, etc.

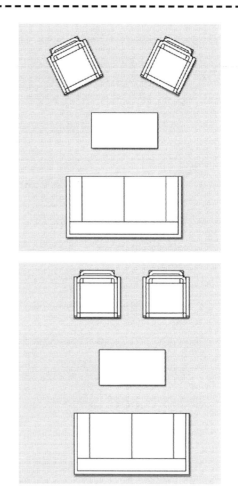

Using a sofa and two armchairs
The armchairs can be easily moved or rotated.

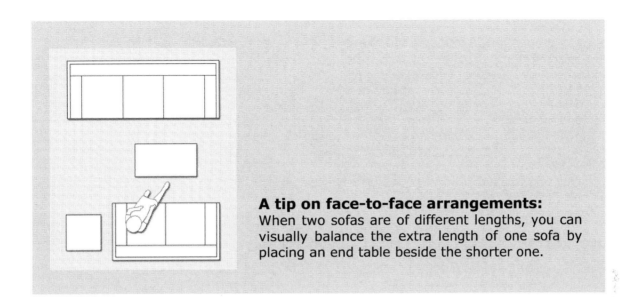

A tip on face-to-face arrangements:
When two sofas are of different lengths, you can visually balance the extra length of one sofa by placing an end table beside the shorter one.

U-Shaped arrangements

In the U-shaped arrangement furniture pieces are placed around the focal point. In the middle of the seating area, a large coffee table or two smaller ones are placed. The U-shape seating group can either float in the center of a room or rest against a wall.

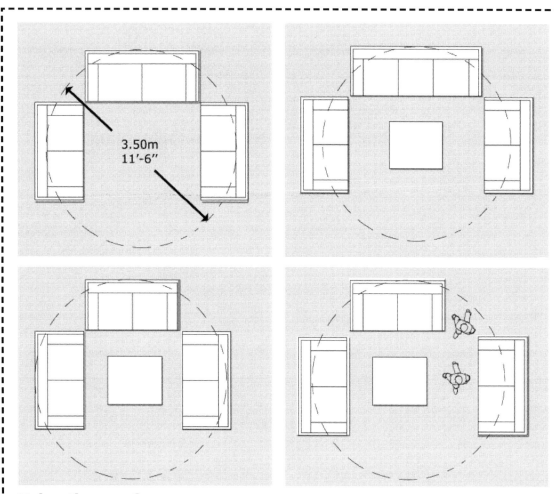

Using three sofas

This arrangement requires plenty of space and you should always be careful not to exceed the maximum allowed conversation distance. All three sofas do not necessarily match; however, it is preferable to create the U section with two matching sofas.

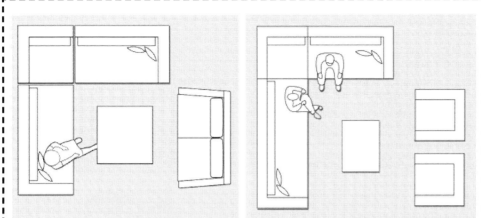

Using a sectional and a loveseat/a sectional and two armchairs

This arrangement takes up a lot of space. It is ideal for large families and those families spending a lot of time in the living room, performing various activities (relaxing, taking a nap, watching TV, having lunch, etc).

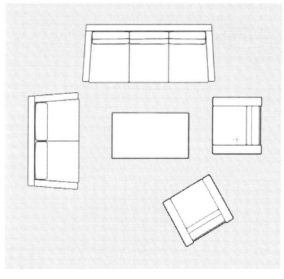

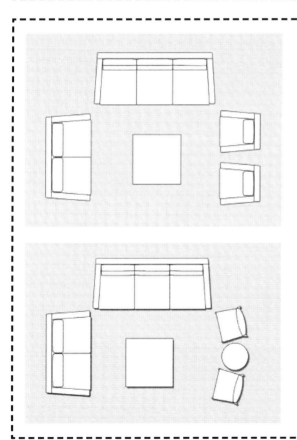

Using two sofas and chairs

The two sofas create an L-shaped seating arrangement complemented by two chairs. An end table may be placed between the chairs creating an additional conversation area.

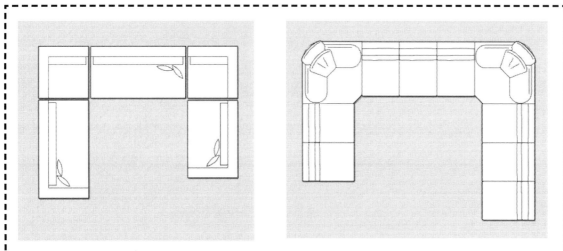

Using sectional sofas
Sectionals are a modular system that can be customized to fit in any living area. However, sectionals in U-shaped arrangement occupy a lot of space.

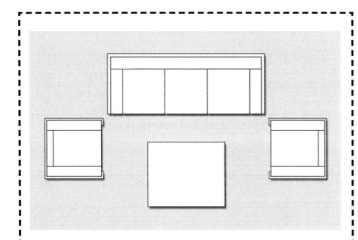

Using a sofa and two armchairs
This arrangement is not recommended for large families or for those inviting friends at home. However, if extra seating is needed floor pillows, ottomans and extra chairs can be used.

Using two sofas and a chaise longue (or a bench)
A bench can substitute the coffee table.

Armchairs in the center of the U-shaped arrangement

A large sofa is not necessarily positioned in the center of the "U". Two armchairs or a chaise longue can be placed instead of the sofa and two identical sofas extend perpendicular to either side of the two armchairs/chaise longue.

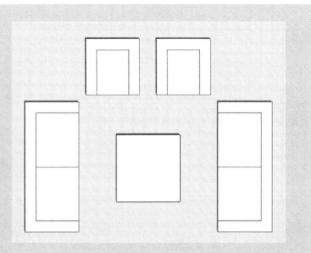

Circulation between sofas

U-shaped arrangements occupy a lot of space in a room. So, there is a possible need to allow circulation paths between furniture. In this case, you should know that furniture placement may be out of the acceptable conversational distance among seaters.

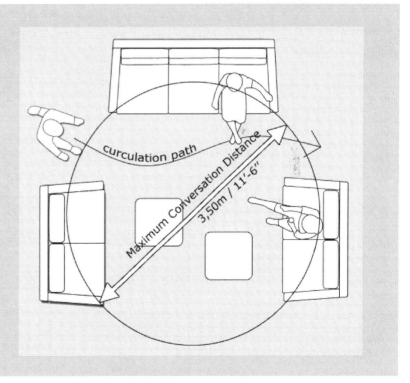

curculation path

Maximum Conversation Distance 3,50m / 11'-6"

Circular arrangement

Circular arrangement encourages comfortable conversation and is preferable when the room lacks a focal point. Some of the furniture pieces should be small and light-weight, for example chairs and ottomans, that can be easily moved away allowing easy access and circulation.

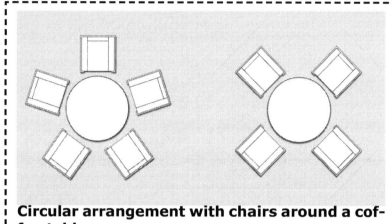

Circular arrangement with chairs around a coffee table

This arrangement allows enjoying tea with friends, eating lunch with family or playing card and board games. It can function as a second seating area.

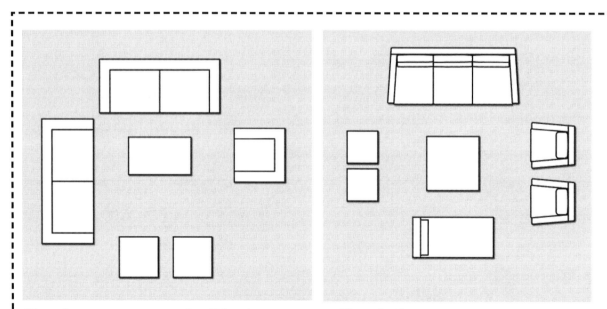

Circular arrangement with ottomans, puffs, chairs, etc

Small sized chairs, such as ottomans, small chairs and puffs, are lightweight, flexible pieces of furniture that can be easily moved and rotated to fulfil needs for temporary seating. They can also complement the main sofa arrangement with additional seating.

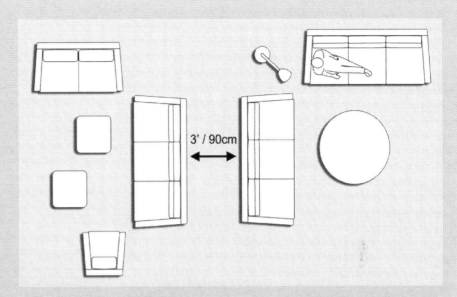

Back-to-Back arrangement in the living room

In a long large space, the back to back placement of two sofas visually divides the room into two seating areas. Allow 2" to 3"/5 to 8cm between the sofas. If you have plenty of space you can position a long narrow console table between the sofas or to leave a pathway at least 3 feet /90cm wide. You don't have to place identical sofas in back-to-back arrangement, especially if there is a pathway between them. If the sofas are a few inches apart, you should choose sofas of similar length and back height. In general, floating a sofa/sectional in the middle of a room can divide an open-plan room to distinct functional areas.

Freestyle and angled arrangement

Small sized lightweight pieces of furniture, such as ottomans, chairs and puffs complement a furniture layout by offering extra seating. They can be easily moved to shape instantly various furniture arrangements, like U-shaped or circular arrangement. Angled furniture placement allows moving pieces away from the wall and can sometimes make a small space seem larger.

TV placement

The TV screen size is related to the distance between the television and the seating. TV manufacturers and retailers recommend that optimum viewing distance is 2.50 times the TV's diagonal size (corresponding to 20-degree viewing angle). This means that buying the largest screen is not always the best choice. However, some argue that HDTVs can be watched at a closer distance, such as 1.5 times the screen's diagonal size (corresponding to 32-degree viewing angle). The longest viewing distance should be 3 or 4 times the TV screen size (the largest the TV screen the longest the distance you can seat).

Regarding the appropriate height for the TV set (on the wall/on a stand), the optimum viewing height is where the center of the screen is at the seated eye level. When the TV set is mounted higher than the recommended height you should ensure that the angle should be no more than 35 degrees above the horizontal plane. For example, mounting the TV above the mantel is not the best option, although it is a common solution; it is not comfortable for your back and neck when sustained for a long period of time. It is preferable to place the TV on the side of the fireplace.

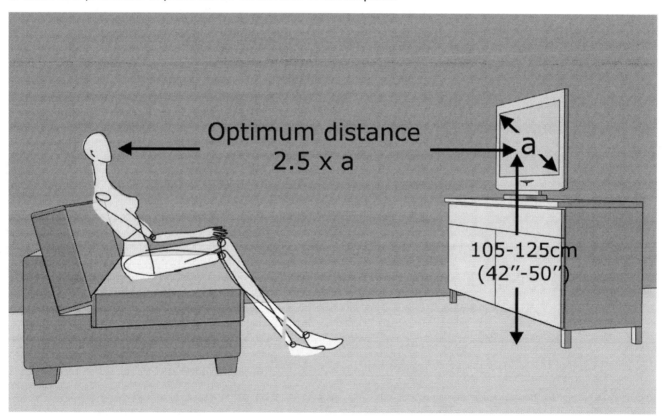

Optimum distance 2.5 x a

a

105-125cm (42"-50")

Viewing distance according to the TV's diagonal size

TOSHIBA Screen Size	Recommended Range	
19"	2.5' – 8.0'	(0.7 – 2.4 m)
22"	3.0' – 9.0'	(0.9 – 2.7 m)
26"	3.5' – 10.5'	(1.0 – 3.1 m)
32"	4.0' – 13.0'	(1.2 – 4.0 m)
37"	4.5' – 15.0'	(1.3 – 4.6 m)
40"	5.0' – 16.5'	(1.5 – 5.0 m)
42"	5.5' – 17.5'	(1.6 – 5.3 m)
46"	6.0' – 19.0'	(1.8 – 5.8 m)
52"	6.5' – 21.5'	(1.9 – 6.5 m)
source: Wikipedia.com		

CRUTCHFIELD		
26"	3.25' – 5.5'	(1.0 m – 1.7 m)
32"	4.0'– 6.66'	(1.2 m – 2.0 m)
37"	4.63' – 7.71'	(1.4 m – 2.4 m)
40"	5.0' – 8.33'	(1.5 m – 2.5 m)
42"	5.25' – 8.75'	(1.6 m – 2.7 m)
46"	5.75' – 9.5'	(1.7 m – 2.9 m)
50"	6.25' – 10.5'	(1.9 m – 3.2 m)
52"	6.5' – 10.8'	(2.0 m – 3.3 m)
55"	6.9' – 11.5'	(2.1 m – 3.5 m)
58"	7.25' – 12.0'	(2.2 m – 3.7 m)
65"	8.13' – 13.5'	(2.5 m – 4.1 m)
70"	8.75' – 14.75'	(2.7 m – 4.5 m)
source: http://www.crutchfield.com		

5. DINING AREA

4. Dining area

A dining room is a room for eating meals. Today, it is usually adjacent either to the kitchen for convenience in serving or to the living room for formal dining with guests or on special occasions. For informal everyday meals, most houses of any size have a space adjacent to the kitchen where table and chairs can be placed.

Usually, a dining room contains a large rectangular dining table with dining chairs; two end chairs are placed at either short side and an even number of side chairs is arranged along the long sides.

In this chapter you will learn:

- The types of dining tables and their standard measurements
- Clearances, optimum distances, allowances, circulation path widths, etc.

Types and measurements of dining tables

The basic concerns when choosing a table are the number of persons you want to accommodate and the available space in the room. However, there are tables having the option to extend their length with leaves that fold out of and back into the table to accommodate extra guests on special occasions.

Square dining table styles

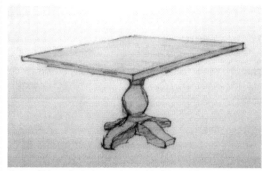
A traditional style pedestal table with carvings

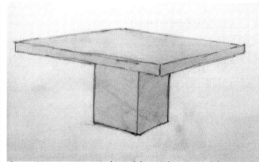
A contemporary style table with central base

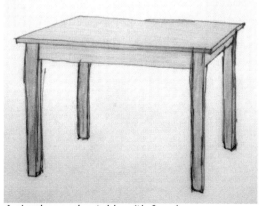
A simple wooden table with four legs

Square dining table measurements

The particular shape encourages dialogue and familiarity between diners and creates a friendly and intimate atmosphere. Small sized square tables usually come with built-in leaf table extends. Dining tables for 2 to 4 people are a common choice as kitchen tables.

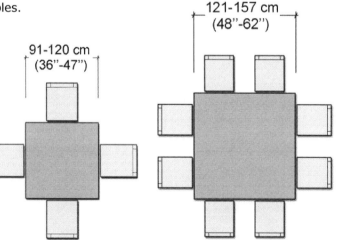

76-90cm
(30"-35")

Up to 2 seaters

91-120 cm
(36"-47")

121-157 cm
(48"-62")

Up to 4 seaters

Up to 8 seaters

Rectangular table typical measurements

Rectangular is the most common shape for dining tables. They are manufactured in a variety of sizes; the number of seaters depends on their size. On the plans below, you can see the typical measurements for comfortable seating. Large rectangular tables can accommodate a large number of seaters; however, they occupy a lot of space.

122-152cm
48"-60"

76-91cm
30"-36"

Up to 4 seaters

152-179cm
60"-70"

76-107cm
30"-47"

Up to 6 seaters

180-239cm
71"-94"

76-107cm
30"-47"

Up to 8 seaters

240-300cm
95"-118"

76-107cm
30"-47"

Up to 10 seaters

241-300cm
95"-118"

122-163cm
48"-64"

Up to 12 seaters

302-358cm'
119"-141"

122-163cm
48"-64"

Up to 14 seaters

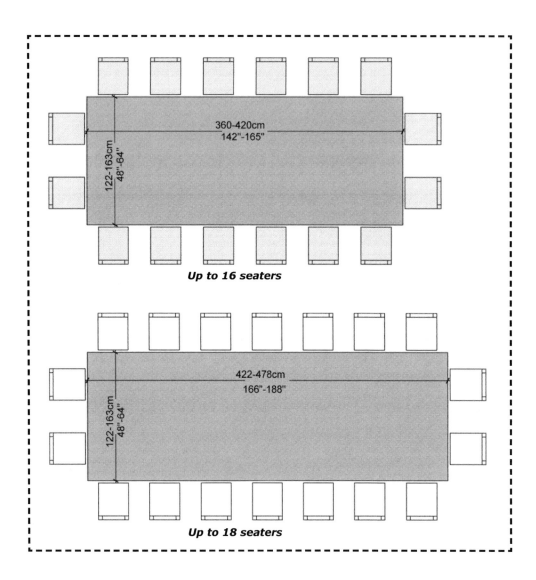

360-420cm
142"-165"

122-163cm
48"-64"

Up to 16 seaters

422-478cm
166"-188"

122-163cm
48"-64"

Up to 18 seaters

Rectangular dining table styles

A simple style rectangular table

An industrial style rectangular table with metal legs

A contemporary style table with an impressive base

An elegant table with glass top and geometric bottom

Round/Oval dining table styles

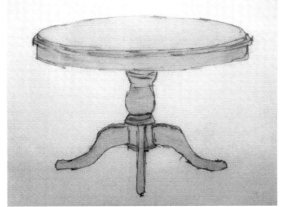

A classic style round table with intricate carvings

An elegant, oval dining table

Round dining table typical measurements

Round tables promote socializing and conversation, since seaters can easily face each other and no one feels isolated. Pedestal tables are a better choice, allowing more seating space around the table. The central leg substitutes the legs around the perimeter that obstruct the chairs. Large round tables are not recommended, since a long radius means that opposite diners seat away from each other and it is difficult to reach the food at the same time. A round table can be converted into an oval with the addition of extension leaves.

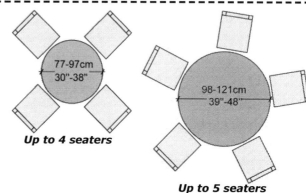

77-97cm
30"-38"
Up to 4 seaters

98-121cm
39"-48"
Up to 5 seaters

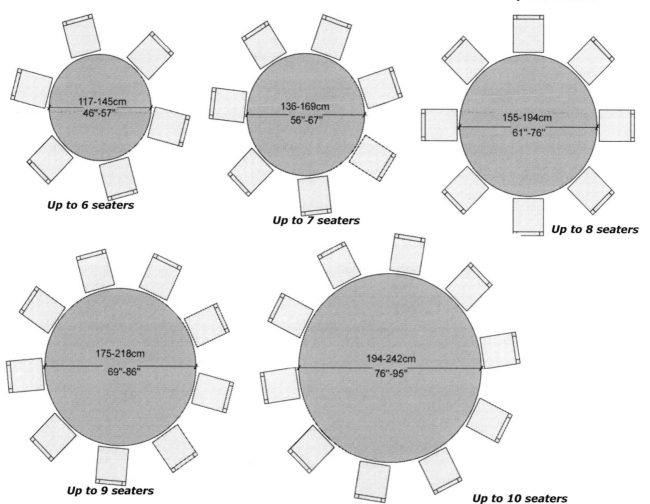

117-145cm
46"-57"
Up to 6 seaters

136-169cm
56"-67"
Up to 7 seaters

155-194cm
61"-76"
Up to 8 seaters

175-218cm
69"-86"
Up to 9 seaters

194-242cm
76"-95"
Up to 10 seaters

Oval dining table typical measurements

An oval table requires almost the same area as a rectangular table. However, it is easier to move and seat around an oval table. Moreover, oval dining tables seem smaller than the rectangular tables due to their rounded corners.

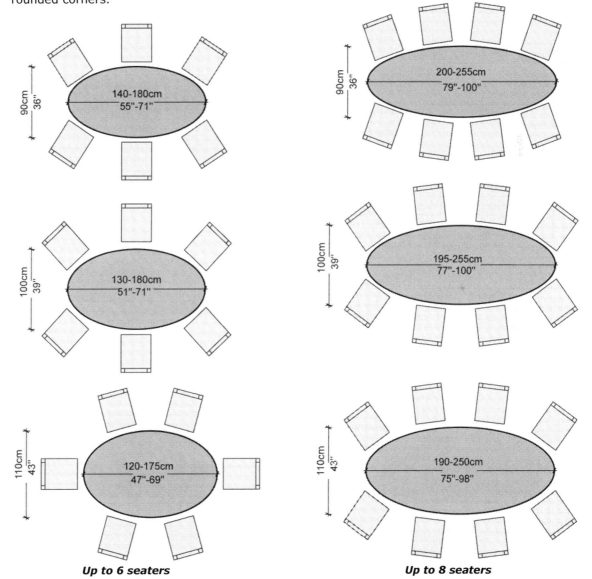

Up to 6 seaters   **Up to 8 seaters**

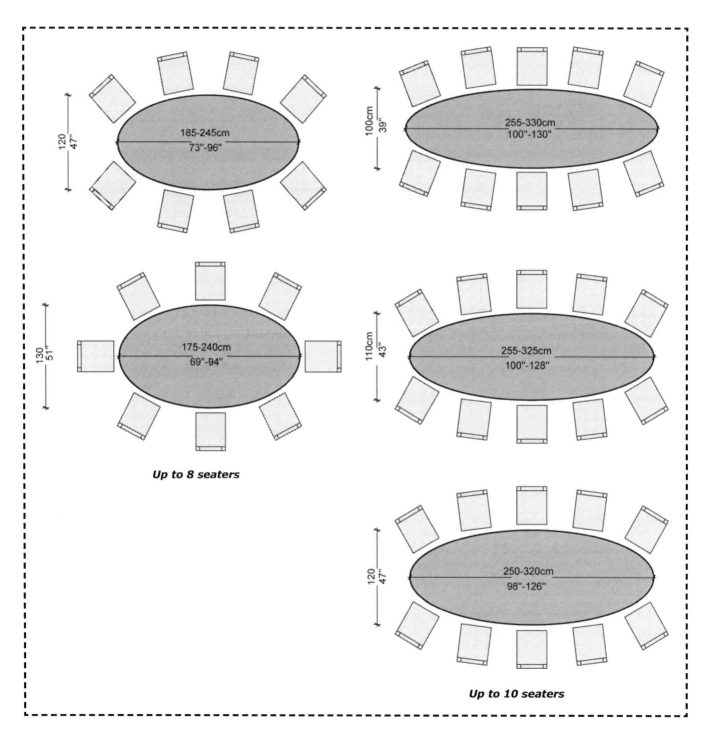

185-245cm
73"-96"

120
47"

255-330cm
100"-130"

100cm
39"

175-240cm
69"-94"

130
51"

255-325cm
100"-128"

110cm
43"

Up to 8 seaters

250-320cm
98"-126"

120
47"

Up to 10 seaters

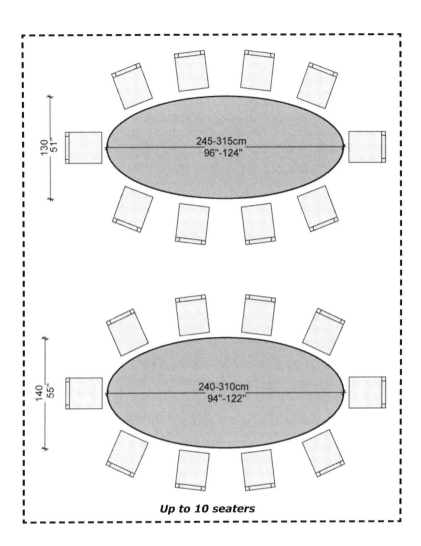

130
51"

245-315cm
96"-124"

140
55"

240-310cm
94"-122"

Up to 10 seaters

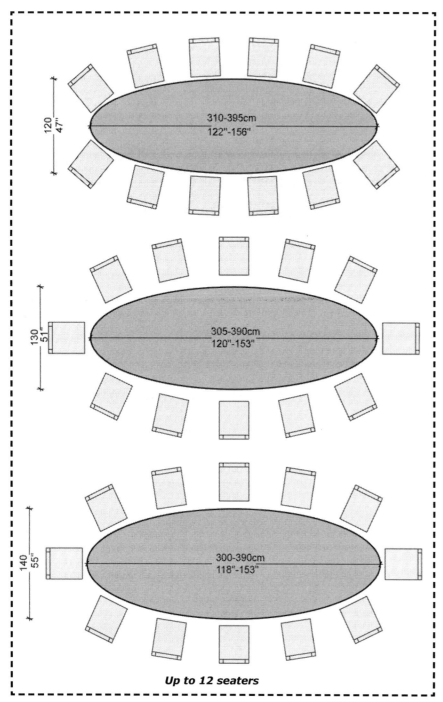

120
47"

310-395cm
122"-156"

130
51"

305-390cm
120"-153"

140
55"

300-390cm
118"-153"

Up to 12 seaters

Calculate the number of seaters that a table can accommodate

In general, a normal diner needs about 61-77cm/24-30 inches of eating space on the tabletop. Thus, by measuring the perimeter of the table you can calculate the number of diners that can be comfortably accommodated. However, in rectangular tables, the rule can be applied only for the long sides; usually, at either opposite short side a single chair is placed.

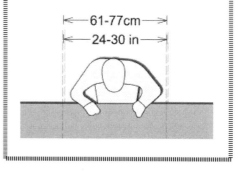

61-77cm
24-30 in

Clearances around the table

Diners may move away from the table several times during a meal. For example, when a person is engaged in casual conversation the chair he is sitting on may be moved a little farther from the table or when a diner stands up the chair may be located even farther away. Thus, a clearance should ensure the diner can eat comfortably, change his body position and stand up.

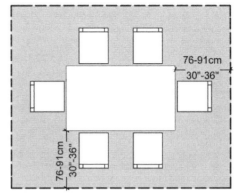

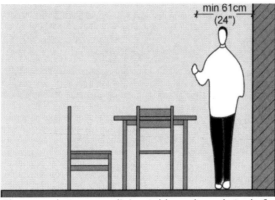

Clearance between a dining table and an obstacle for passage only (no sitting)

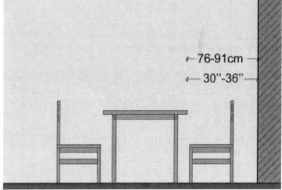

Clearance between a chair and an obstacle when there is no circulation in-between

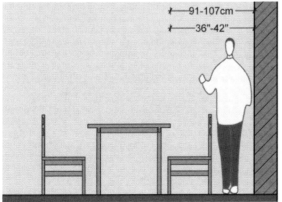

Clearance between a dining table and an obstacle when there is restricted circulation behind a chair. This will require a person to sidestep or the seated person to adjust his chair to allow passage

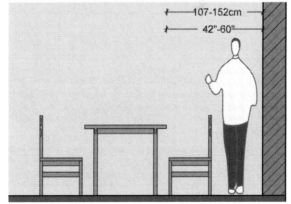

Clearance between a chair and an obstacle providing unrestricted circulation and serving

Clearances between table and storage cabinets

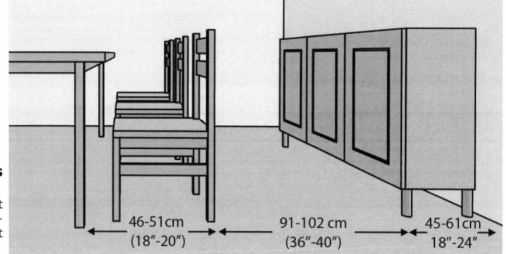

Storage cabinets with doors
Clearance requirement depends on the opening width of the cabinet doors

46-51cm
(18"-20")

91-102 cm
(36"-40")

45-61cm
18"-24"

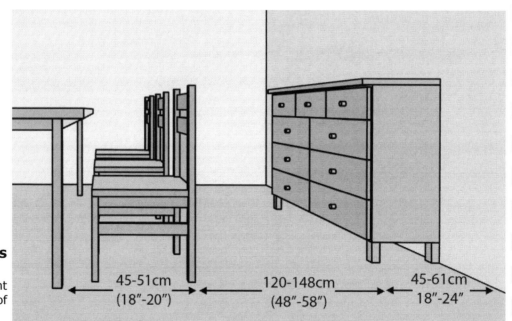

Storage cabinets with drawers
Clearance requirement depends on the width of the drawer opening

45-51cm
(18"-20")

120-148cm
(48"-58")

45-61cm
18"-24"

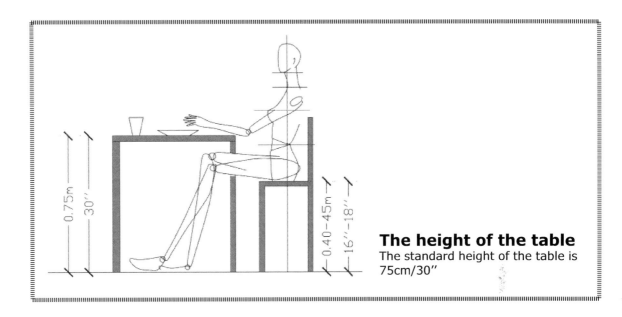

The height of the table
The standard height of the table is 75cm/30"

6. STORAGE & STUDYING AREA

6. Storage & studying area

Typical storage furniture in the living/dining room are bookcases, cabinets, chests of drawers and even ottomans and coat racks.

In this chapter you will learn:

- The most common storage and study pieces of furniture and their measurements
- The required clearances in front of each piece

Types of Bookcases

Shelf bookcase
It is the most common type of bookcase. It can be open-backed or close-backed with adjustable shelves that vary from two to six or more. It can be freestanding or built into a wall.

Step back cabinet
It is made up of two cabinets, a base cabinet and a hutch not as deep as the base on top of it.

Barrister bookcase
It is a bookcase whose shelves are enclosed behind doors with glass panels, for books and items that need protection. The doors lift up and slide into the unit to open each cabinet.

Cabinet bookcase
It is similar to a barrister bookcase. The difference between them is the way the doors of each bookcase open. The doors of the cabinet bookcase open outward from the center.

Modular bookcase
It is constructed from individual units that are stack horizontally and vertically. It does not have a back and it can be a freestanding item or a framed piece that is hanged on a wall.

Folding bookcase
It is a shelving system that can be folded; thus, it can be moved without being disassembled.

Ladder bookcase
It resembles a ladder with shelves, the number of which varies from four to eight; the shelves have no back. It can be freestanding or leaning against a wall.

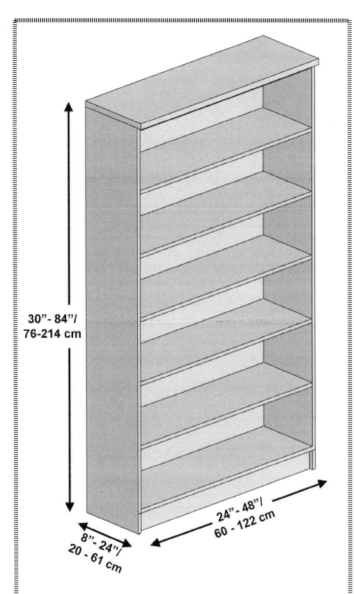

30"- 84"/
76-214 cm

24" - 48"/
60 - 122 cm

8" - 24"/
20 - 61 cm

Bookcase typical measurements

A bookcase or a bookshelf, is a piece of furniture with shelves, used to store books, relevant printed material and decorative items. Some bookcase have glass doors to protect the books from dust.

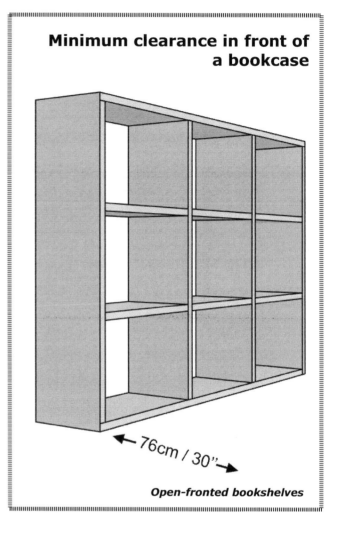

Minimum clearance in front of a bookcase

76cm / 30"

Open-fronted bookshelves

Storage cabinets - Clearances

A cabinet is a box-shaped furniture piece with doors or drawers serving storage purposes. Cabinets normally have one or two opening doors on the front; some others may have drawers and doors or only sets of drawers. Floor cabinets may have a finished top surface that can be used as a working area. Clearance in front of a cabinet is necessary allowing the doors and drawers to open properly and the user to comfortably reach stored items.

Cabinets with drawers

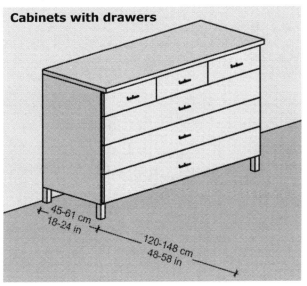

45-61 cm
18-24 in

120-148 cm
48-58 in

Cabinet with doors

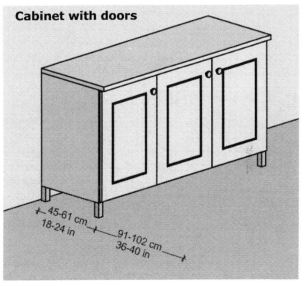

45-61 cm
18-24 in

91-102 cm
36-40 in

Typical measurements

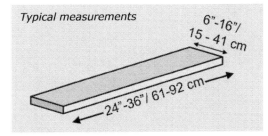

6"-16"/
15 - 41 cm

24"-36"/ 61-92 cm

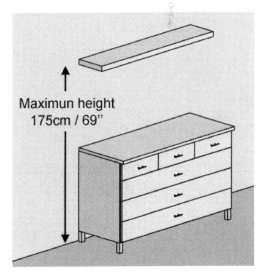

Maximun height
175cm / 69"

Shelves

A shelf is a flat horizontal structure which holds various items for display or simply storage purposes. It is raised off the ground and attached to the wall or other vertical surface with wall brackets. A floating shelf is attached on hidden internal brackets. The length of a shelf defines the load it can bear. The maximum reaching height of a shelf to be installed depends on the user's height; this means that shelves above 175cm/69" are difficult to be reached.

Writing desk
It resembles a dining table and includes one to three small drawers at the top for letters and other paper documents.

Computer desk
It is a desk constructed especially for a desktop computer housing its accessories. There are not many drawers, as the user stores everything on the computer.

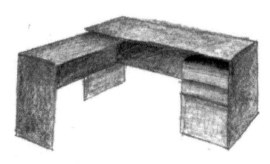

Executive desk
It is a combination of a writing desk and a computer desk. It can be rectangular, L-shaped or C-shaped for those who need lots of work space.

Pedestal desk
It is a type of executive desk with pedestals on each side. The pedestals are usually sets of drawers. Often, there is a central drawer at the top.

Slant-front desk
It is a desk similar to secretary desk without the bookcase.

Roll-top desk
It is a rectangular executive desk or a pedestal desk with a hutch which also includes a roll-top.

Secretary desk
It is a writing desk with a hutch or a set of drawers on top. A flat surface folds up and down to create a desk space whenever it is needed.

Desks: Clearances
A typical study area may include a desk with a chair, a computer, and a bookcase or bookshelves. A spare bedroom is often used as a study room, although many contemporary homes have a room designated for that purpose. In case there is not a spare room, you can create a study area into the living room. Clearance behind the desk should be adequate for comfortable sitting and working.

The desk can be arranged overlooking a window to get some privacy or placed at an angle in a corner overlooking the room; leaving enough space between the desk and the wall enables reaching the seat.

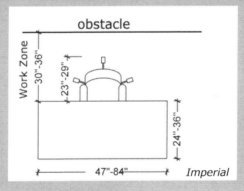

Imperial

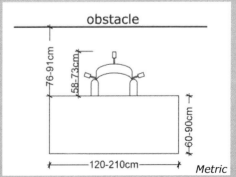

Metric

Desk measurements

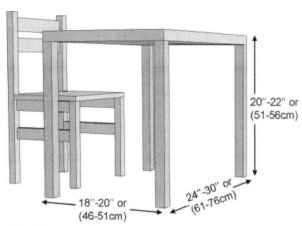

20"-22" or
(51-56cm)

18"-20" or
(46-51cm)

24"-30" or
(61-76cm)

Childrens desk

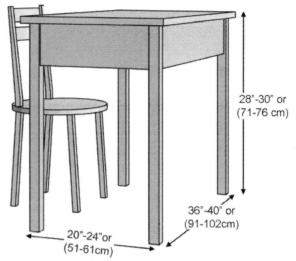

28"-30" or
(71-76 cm)

36"-40" or
(91-102cm)

20"-24"or
(51-61cm)

Writing table

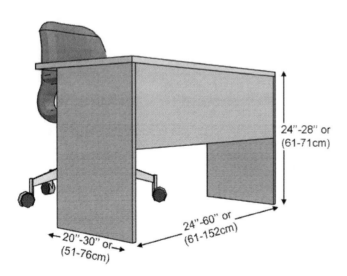

24"-28" or
(61-71cm)

20"-30" or
(51-76cm)

24"-60" or
(61-152cm)

Computer desk

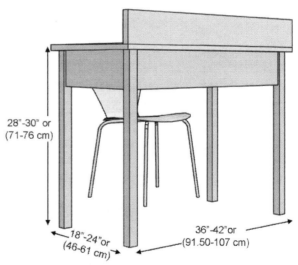

28"-30" or
(71-76 cm)

18"-24"or
(46-61 cm)

36"-42"or
(91.50-107 cm)

Secretary/Slant front desk

Chair measurements

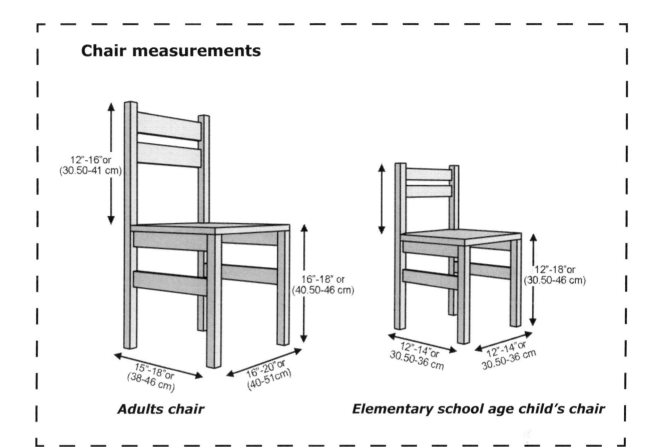

12"-16"or
(30.50-41 cm)

16"-18" or
(40.50-46 cm)

15"-18"or
(38-46 cm)

16"-20"or
(40-51cm)

Adults chair

12"-18"or
(30.50-46 cm)

12"-14"or
30.50-36 cm

12"-14"or
30.50-36 cm

Elementary school age child's chair

---

7. ARRANGING ART ON WALLS

7. Arranging art on walls

Artwork on walls adds character and makes the space intriguing. Art and furniture are of the same importance, as paintings give a tone to any room. Artwork (paintings, photographs, etc) arrangement on a blank wall is not always obvious, as it requires experimenting, imagination and reflection. The process becomes even more complicated if the artworks are numerous and of different types and sizes.

You should consider a number of parameters, such as the height an artwork should be hung on the wall, the type of grouping of the pictures on the wall, the size of paintings, and the kind of room an artwork will be hung so as to decide how and where to hang it.

In this chapter you'll learn:

- How to arrange artwork above the sofa in the living room
- How to arrange artwork above the headboard in the bedroom

117

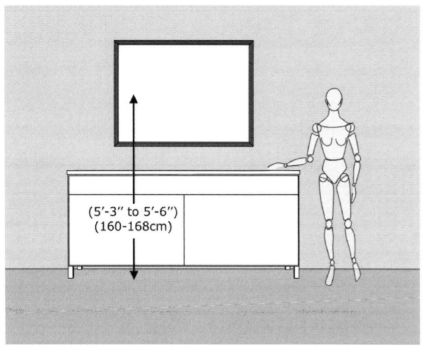

(5'-3" to 5'-6")
(160-168cm)

At what height an artwork should be hung?

Artwork should be hung so that the center point of the piece of art or the grouping is at proximately an average person's eye level, which is between 5'-3" and 5'-6"/157cm and 165cm. In case you have a group of pictures you should consider them as one larger picture.

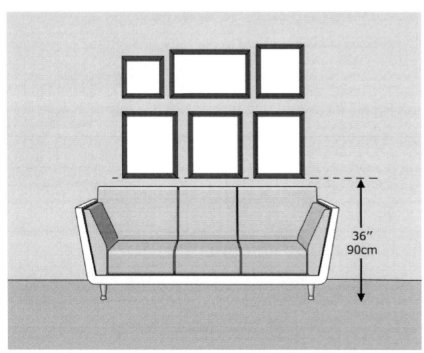

36"
90cm

Minimum height for artwork placement

Artwork should be displayed prominently on walls and users must be able to comfortably see it without stretching or kneeling. So, you should avoid placing artwork at a height lower than 36"/90cm.

Art on the living room walls

A common place to hang artwork is above the sofa provided that it is placed against a wall. Another fine place could be above the fireplace. The first step is the careful observation of the paintings, so as to decide which ones to be placed on the walls. If there are many available, it is obvious not every painting can be placed, but some of them can be stored for future use.

A careful observation of the mat board types, the picture frame types and sizes, the paintings' theme, etc leads to some initial thoughts on a possible artwork placement. For example, an important artwork, even if it is small in size, can be hung on its own on a wall.

The following artwork placement guide takes into account geometry and the picture size without taking notice of the themes and the paintings' artistic value. The guide concerns hanging art pieces above the sofa, although these rules can be used when placing artwork at different positions.

Symmetrical placement
It is probably the most common and "safe" placement, as it helps the visitor to focus on a particular point. It is ideal for pictures of similar size and shape and creates a grouping which has purity, visual balance and harmony. The symmetrical artwork placement is perfect above large furniture and it is usually created by placing a large piece in the middle and some smaller pieces around it to form a unit.

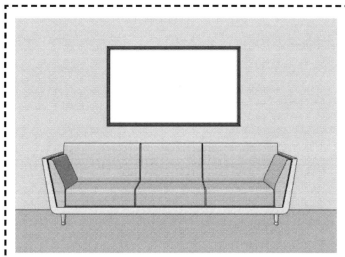

Central placement with one painting

It is suitable for large size pieces which are of great importance. These pieces should be placed to the focal point of the room, usually the fireplace, to draw the attention.

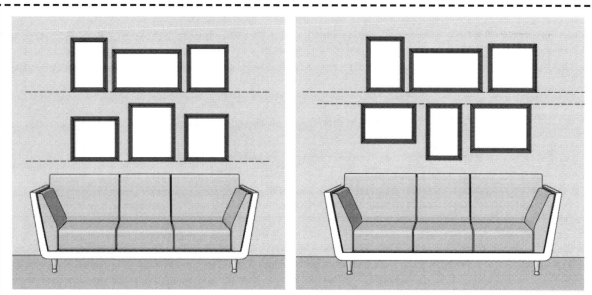

Horizontal alignment

Horizontal alignment elongates and "extends" the width of a narrow room. You can choose one row or two rows layout, in case of small height paintings. The standard one row layout is to align their centers. Alternatively you can align their top or bottom edges for a more contemporary look.

If you have frames of different heights you can choose to arrange them in two rows aligning the edges instead of aligning their centers. This arrangement is appropriate for paintings of different size, type, theme or frame as well. You can group them to create an interesting composition.

Centered on both the horizontal and the vertical axes

You can organize paintings of similar size using both horizontal and vertical center alignment for a sense of balance and symmetry.

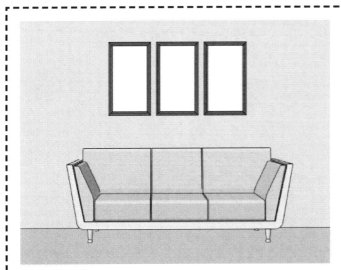

Triptychs

A triptych is a work in three related panels displayed together making one art piece. Alternatively it can be composed of artworks similar in color combination, theme, and frame style displayed side by side. In this case the panels should be of the same size.

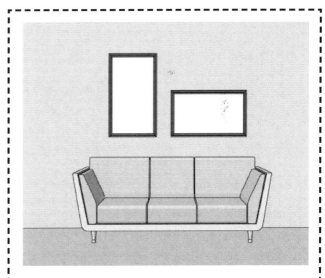

One horizontal and one vertical artwork in combination

One vertical and one horizontal piece of art can be placed side by side aligned based on their bottom edges.

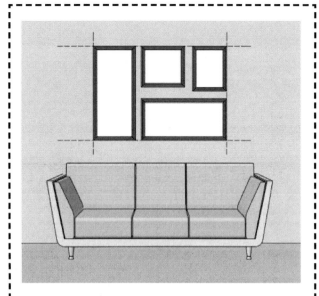

Geometrical arrangement

All pieces of art are contained within an imaginary geometric shape, i.e. a rectangle. Larger pieces should be placed in proper positions and smaller ones fill the vacancies. This arrangement allows plenty of freedom in mixing different shapes of paintings.

Grouping by size

Due to this arrangement grouping of smaller pieces is combined with a large painting so as to create balance and interest.

Asymmetrical arrangement

This arrangement requires high synthesis perception and provides an interesting and vivid look. The artworks are placed unevenly producing a harmonic result.

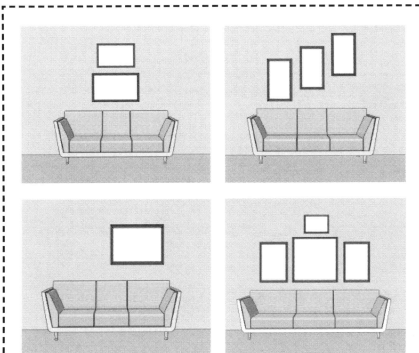

Don'ts when placing art-work

Some kinds of artwork arrangements should be avoided, as they are considered outdated or incoherent. For example, the painting arrangement in diagonal lines over the sofa or paintings one above the other or aligned with one edge of the sofa should be avoided.

Notice:
Artwork should be related to wall and furniture size, i.e. small pictures should be placed on narrow walls and large ones on bigger walls. Moreover, artwork should not exceed furniture width. Generally the artwork should be about 75% the width of the furniture.

Tips:
You can make a template of each artwork using brown cardboard. You can move them on the wall experimenting with their position until your layout is perfect. Thus, you will not make multiple nail holes on the walls.

Frequent change in the artwork location on the walls refreshes the room and makes the wall art remarkable again, as you've got used to the previous position. You can also consider a new arrangement of your artwork.

Art on bedroom walls

A bedroom is a place for relaxation, so it should promote harmony and tranquillity. Artwork can be hung over the bed or on an opposite wall. The bed is the focal point of a bedroom; consequently the wall behind it should be featured. In case the headboard is small or nonexistent, a large artwork or a grouping of smaller ones can create an interesting headboard alternative. Artwork arrangement options mentioned before can be followed to hang pieces on bedroom walls.

A large square artwork above the headboard

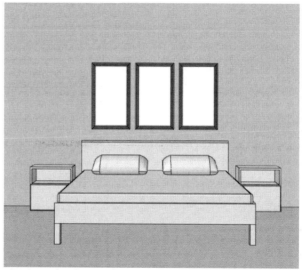

A triptych above the headboard

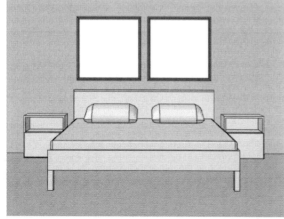

Two pieces of artwork above the headboard

Artworks above the headboard

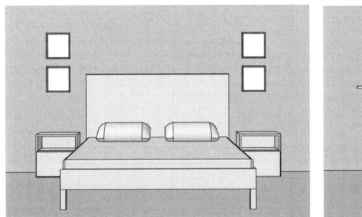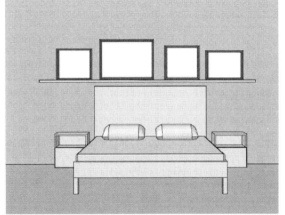

What to do when you have a large headboard

A big headboard can stand on its own, consequently you should avoid hanging something above it. You can hang artwork above the bedside tables or you can construct a long shelf for artwork placement instead.

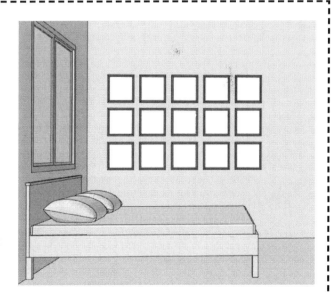

Tip:
If there is an empty wall in the bedroom (usually, this happens when the bed is placed in front of the window), you can create a small artwork gallery on this empty wall.

8. BEDROOMS
IIIIIIIIIIIIIIIIIIIIIIIIIIIII
IIIIIIIIIIIIIIIIIIIIIIIIIIII
IIIIIIIIIIIIIIIIIIIIIIIIIIIIIII

8. Bedrooms

The bedroom is the most private space in which we spend about a third of our lives. It is primarily used for relaxing, reflecting, sleeping, loving, dressing/undressing etc. A bedroom is also used for more activities, such as reading, studying, watching TV, listening to music, personal care etc.
It is therefore essential that a bedroom should be a well-organized space with the right furniture placement.
Although the bedroom décor style should express its occupant's personality and preferences, there are some standards in furniture placement in a bedroom in order to be functional and comfortable.

Furniture can be arranged in many ways but some basic factors are the age of the occupants, which immediately defines the bedroom type (master bedroom, children's bedroom etc), the number and gender of the occupants (necessary for children's bedroom), the size and shape of the bedroom, the location of the entry door, the patio door or the windows, the size and the type of furniture, the space allowance and clearances, the storage space for clothes, toys etc.

In this chapter, you will learn:
-Types of bedrooms
-Bedroom furniture
-Bedroom furniture dimensions
-Bedroom clearances
-Furniture arrangement basics
-Bedrooms layouts

Bed types

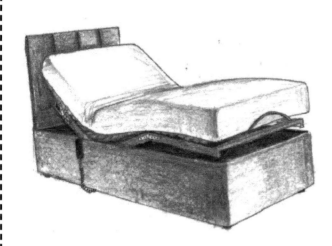

Adjustable bed
An adjustable bed has a metal base with an electric motor, which using a remote control raises and lowers the head and the foot of the bed in different positions.

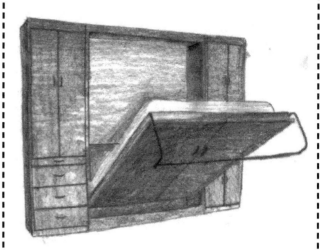

Murphy bed
A Murphy bed is a bed that folds up vertically against a wall or into a storage cabinet.

Box bed
A box bed is a bed with storage space underneath.

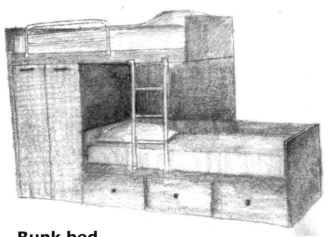

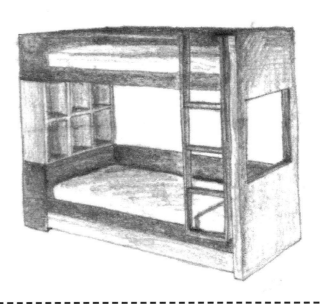

Bunk bed

A bunk bed is a unit of two single beds that are stuck firmly on each other. A ladder allows one sleeper to use the top bunk.

Canopy bed/four poster bed

A canopy bed (commonly four-poster bed) is a bed with four tall posts on each corner which support a rectangular panel on the top.

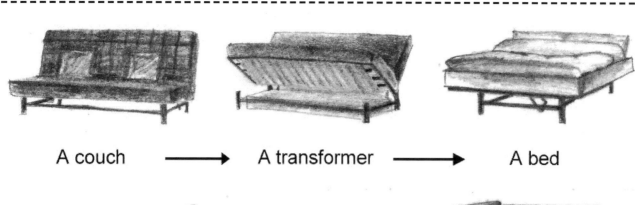

A couch ➡️ A transformer ➡️ A bed

Couch bed/Sofa bed
It is a couch (sofa) that can be converted into a bed.

Trundle bed
A trundle bed is a bed that can be moved to fit under another bed.

Sleigh bed
It is a bed with headboard and footboard that are curled outward to resemble a sleigh.

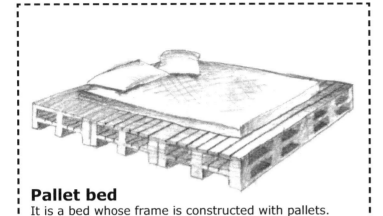

Pallet bed
It is a bed whose frame is constructed with pallets.

Loft bed
Loft bed is an elevated bed that leaves free space underneath for placing other furniture, such as a desk.

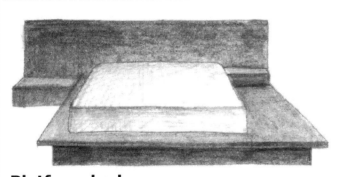

Platform bed
A platform bed is a bed with a flat platform on which the mattress is placed.

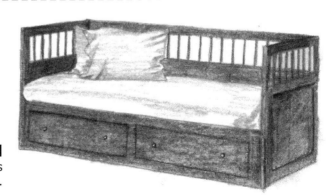

Daybed
A daybed is a bed that is used as a bed and as a sofa.

Bedside table types

There are 3 different types of bedside tables; they all have the same function but they slightly differ in use.

Bedside chest

A bedside chest includes 2 or 3 drawers which provide extra storage.

Bedside cabinet

A bedside cabinet includes a cabinet and a drawer above it.

Nightstand

A nightstand includes only one drawer for storage and its function is mainly to provide a stand for putting an alarm clock or a bedside lamp.

Beds & Mattresses dimensions

The bed size refers to the mattress dimensions. The bed sizes vary according to the size of the frame and the decoration. However, they are sold according to the mattress that fits onto the bed's frame. The standard bed sizes vary by the country and the measurement system each one uses, as seen below. Commercial bedding sets fit the standard sizes of mattresses.

BED TYPE	Size in inches (width X length)	Size in cm (width X length)	sleepers
Standard Bunk Bed Size	39" X 75"	99.10 x 190.50 cm	1
Narrow Bunk Bed Size	36" X 75"	91.40 X 190.50 cm	1
Twin Bed Size / Single Bed Size	39" X 75"	99.10 X 190.50 cm	1
Twin Extra Long Bed Size	39" X 80"	99.10 X 203.20 cm	1
Full Bed Size/ Double Bed Size	54" X 75"	137.20 X 190.50 cm	2
Queen Bed Size	60" X 80"	152.40 X 203.20 cm	2
California Queen Bed Size	60" X 84"	152.40 X 213.40 cm	2
Expanded Queen Bed Size	66" X 80"	167.60 X 203.20 cm	2
Super Queen Bed Size	66" X 80"	167.60 X 203.20 cm	2
King Bed Size	76" X 80"	193.00 X 203.20 cm	2
California King Bed Size	72" X 84"	182.90 X 213.40 cm	2
Grand King Bed Size	80" X 98"	203.20 X 248.90 cm	2

USA Bed and Mattress Dimensions

BED TYPE	Size in inches (width X length)	Size in cm (width X length)	sleepers
Single Bed Size	36" X 75"	91.40 X 190.50 cm	1
Bunk Bed Size	36" X 75"	91.40 X 190.50 cm	1
Double Bed Size	54" X 75"	137.20 X 190.50 cm	2
King Bed Size	60" X 78"	152.40 X 198.10 cm	2
Super King Bed Size	72" X 78"	182.90 X 198.10 cm	2
		UK Bed and Mattress Sizes	

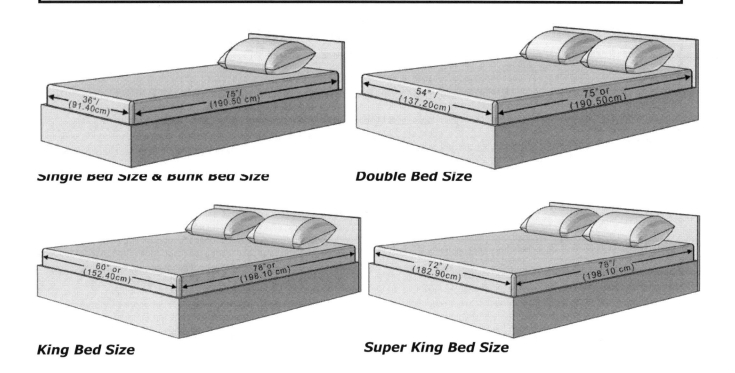

Single Bed Size & Bunk Bed Size

Double Bed Size

King Bed Size

Super King Bed Size

Important Notice: The bed sizes mentioned in this book refer to the mattress dimensions. The actual bed measurements vary according to the size of the frame and the decoration.

134

Juvenile bed & Mattresses dimensions

BED TYPE	Size in inches (width X length)	Size in cm (width X length)	sleepers
Bassinet	(18"-27") X (27"-45")	(45.72-68.58) X (68.58-114.30) cm	1
Cradle	(12"-22") X (28"-36")	(30.48-55.88) X (71.12-91.44) cm	1
Junior crib	(23"-25") X (46"-50")	(58.42-63.50) X (116.80-127.00) cm	1
6-year crib	(27"-31") X (51"-56")	(68.58-78.74 X 129.50-142.20) cm	1
Youth bed	(33"-36") X (66"-76")	(83.82-91.44) X (167.60-193.00) cm	2
Playpen	(23"-30") X (40"-47")	(58.42-76.20) X (101.60-119.40) cm	2

Bedroom furniture measurements range

FURNITURE	Size in inches (width X length X height)	Size in cm (width X length X height)
Bedside tables	(24"-26") X (16''-19'') X (24"-30")	(60.96-66.04) X (40.64-48.26) X (60.96-76.20) cm
Changing table	(32"-48") X (17"-22") X (36"-40")	(81.28-121.90) X (43.18-55.88) X (91.44-101.60) cm
Chest of drawers (bureau)	(32"-40") X (18"-22") X (42"-56")	(81.28-101.60) X (45.72-55.88) X (106.70-142.20) cm
Dresser	(36"-48") X (18"-24") X (29"-37")	(91.44-121.90) X (45.72-60.96) X (73.66-93.98) cm
Double dresser	(60"-72") X (18"-22") X (26"-34")	(152.40-182.90) X (45.72-55.88) X (66.04-86.30) cm
Bedroom vanity	(30"-82") X (16"-20") X (30"-70")	(76.20-208.30) X (40.64-50.80) X (76.20-177.80) cm
Step back cabinet	(36"-48") X (10"-13") X (72"-84")	(91.44-121.90) X (25.40-33.02) X (182.90-213.40) cm

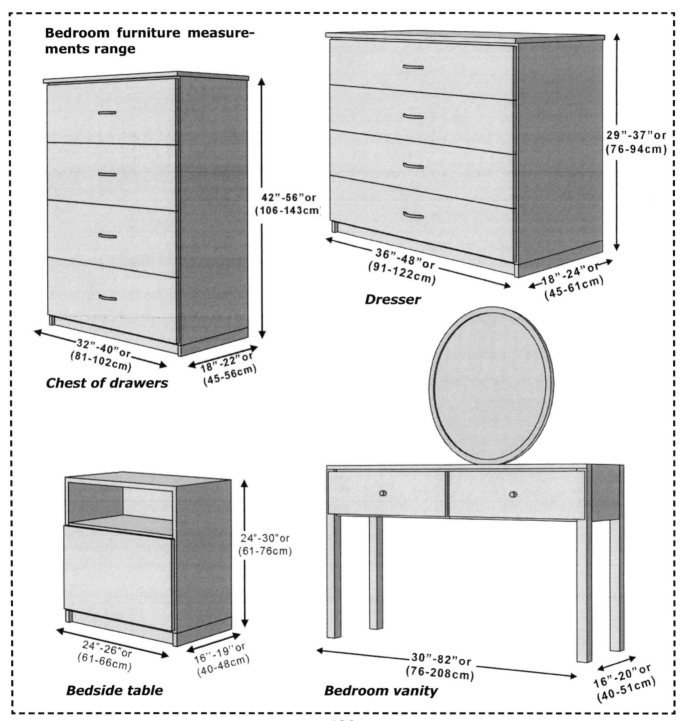

Bedroom furniture measurements range

42"-56"or
(106-143cm)

32"-40"or
(81-102cm)

18"-22"or
(45-56cm)

Chest of drawers

29"-37"or
(76-94cm)

36"-48"or
(91-122cm)

18"-24"or
(45-61cm)

Dresser

24"-30"or
(61-76cm)

24"-26"or
(61-66cm)

16"-19"or
(40-48cm)

Bedside table

30"-82"or
(76-208cm)

16"-20"or
(40-51cm)

Bedroom vanity

Clearances in the bedroom

Some bedroom space should be available for walking, making the bed, using the dressers, the closets, etc. The minimum clearances in a bedroom should be as following:

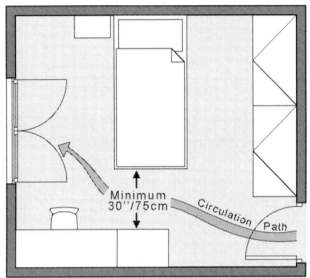

Main circulation path: The main walking path from the door through the room should be at least 30"/76cm wide.

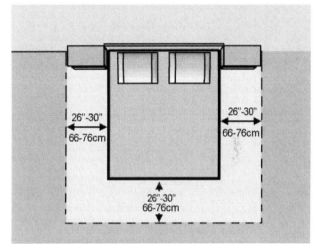

Clearance around the bed: The bedroom layout should give clearance of 26"-30" (66-76cm) around the bed. Clearance is important to allow bed-making and circulation around the bed.

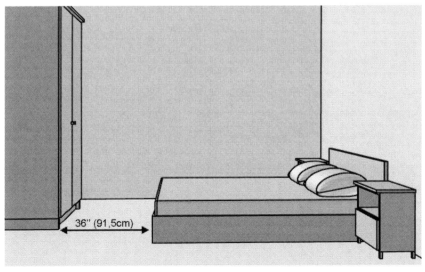

Clearance in front of a wardrobe or in front of a chest of drawers: If there is a wardrobe or dresser standing parallel to the bed, allow clearance of 36" (91,5 cm) between the side of the bed and the other item.

If there isn't enough space available for this kind of placement, follow this guideline: Measure the width of the wardrobe door and increase that by 4"/10cm. This is the distance you should leave between the closet and the bed.

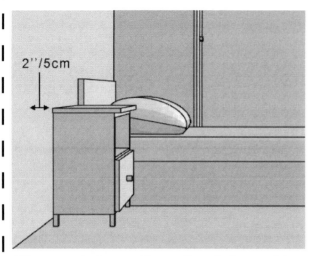

Allowance between the wall and pieces of furniture: The distance between the wall and a piece of furniture should be 2"/5cm. This prevents damages to the furniture and protects the wall from scratches and accidents caused by abrupt contact.

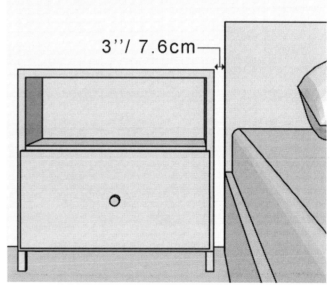

Allowance between pieces of furniture: The distance between pieces of furniture should be 3"/7.6cm.

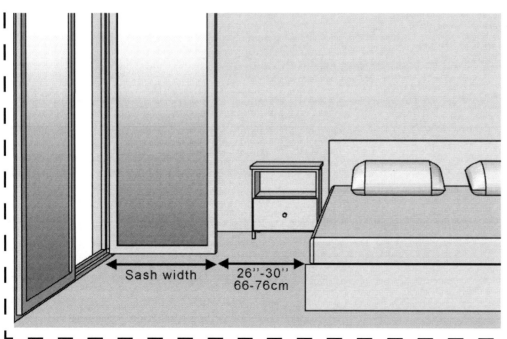

If there is a patio door in the room the distance between the bed and the wall with the patio door/window should be increased by the width of the sash.

Clearance between two single beds. The minimum distance between two single beds should be 24"/ 61 cm. Of course the largest the distance the easiest the circulation and access.

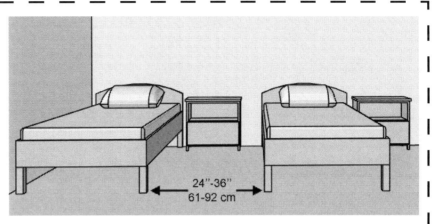

24"-36"
61-92 cm

If there is enough free space, on one side of each bed then the clearance between the two beds could be smaller, 20"/51cm, since there is no need for circulation between the two beds, apart from the placement of a bedside table in-between.

Minimum
free space 36" (91 cm)

20"-24"
51-61cm

Minimum
free space 36" (91 cm)

Examples of bedroom layouts with minimum clearances

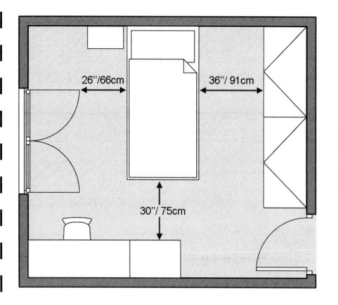

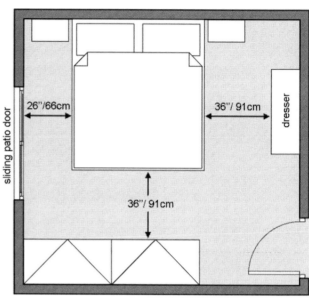

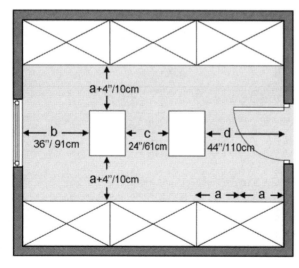

Clearances in a walk-in closet

a= The closet door width. The open space width should be increased by 4"/ 10cm.
b= Open space width in front of a dresser.
c= Secondary circulation path. Open space width around the island of the walk-in closet.
d= Distance between entry door and obstacle.

Single bed position

The position of the bed in a room has a major impact on its functionality and decoration. Generally, when arranging bedroom furniture, the largest piece is arranged first and the additional pieces are placed around it. A single bed can be placed:

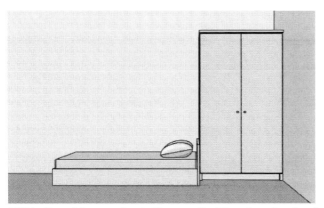

With its side against the wall. *The drawback of this placement is that you cannot place a bedside table next to the side of the bed. However, you can place a large piece of furniture, such as a wardrobe/desk behind the headboard.*

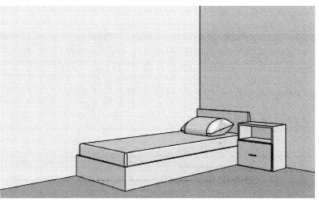

In a corner. *It is the most advantageous placement for small bedrooms where the available space is limited.*

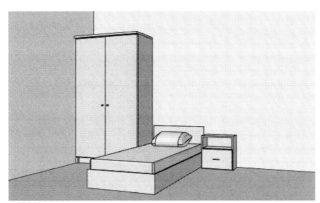

With its head to the wall. *A basic option, where the bed is perpendicular to the longest wall and the headboard faces the room. The advantage is that you get three free sides of the bed.*

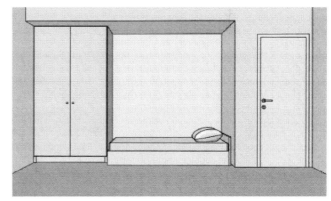

In a an alcove.

How to arrange twin beds in a room

Usually, two children or guests have to share the same room and co-exist. In these situations, the main dilemma is always the bed placement. However, there is more than one way to organize a multi-person bedroom. Below, we have illustrated almost all possible solutions and combinations. However, all solutions are not suitable for every space. Each room has its own restrictions, regarding dimensions and proportions, the location of the entry door, the windows, the closet, etc.

Create an L-shaped arrangement by placing the two beds in a corner of the room. It is preferable to keep an empty space between the beds, and place in the corner or in-between a piece of furniture, such as a wardrobe, a desk, a table or a nightstand. You can place the beds, footboard-to-footboard, headboard-to-headboard or headboard-to-footboard.

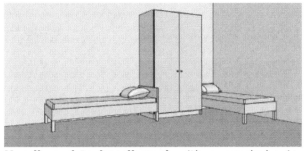

Headboard-to-headboard *with a wardrobe in-between. The wardrobe adds privacy to each individual bed.*

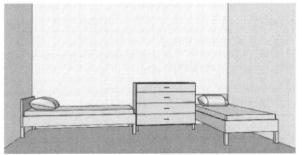

Headborad-to-foorboard *with a dresser in-bewteen. The dresser also serves as a nightstand.*

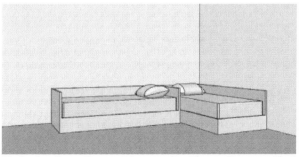

Twin beds adjacent to each other. *Be sure that the bed design allows this arrangement.*

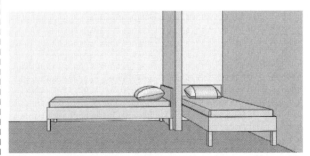

The drywall shaft wall corner *column offers privacy to the occupants and creates distinct areas.*

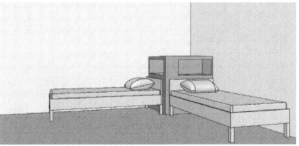

Headborad-to-headboard placement *with a custom made, built-in furniture.*

With the headboards on the same wall (parallel placement).

Both beds are placed perpendicular to the longest wall with the headboards facing the room's interior. Usually a nightstand or two nightstands are placed in-between. Alternatively, you can place a wardrobe or a dresser in-between. Placing the beds next to each other to make a large bed is an option suitable only for small kids, since as a child grows up needs more personal space.

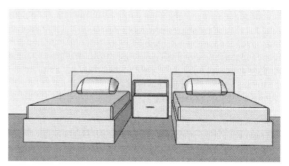

Parallel bed arrangement with a nightstand in-between.

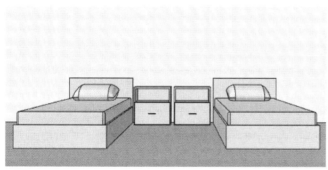

Parallel bed arrangement with two nightstands, a dresser or a wardrobe in-between.

Beds placement, next to each other.

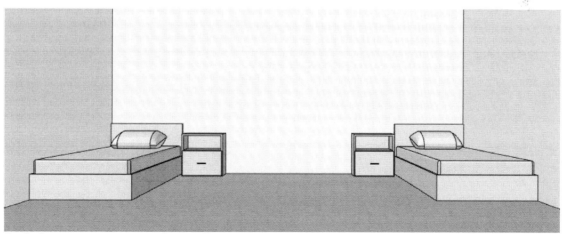

Bed placement on opposite walls. Occupants have extra room in the middle to move around.

Both beds with their long sides against the wall.

You can place the beds either adjacent to each other or leaving free space between them. Of course the wall should be long enough to accommodate both beds.

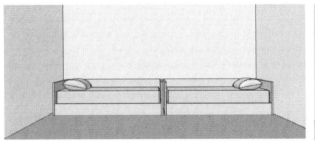

Footboard-to-footboard placement.

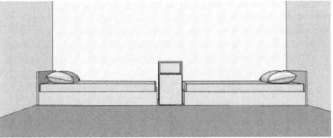

Footboard-to-footboard placement with a piece of furniture in-between.

With headboards along opposite walls and/or in opposite corners.

To maximize personal space you can place the beds along opposite walls and in opposite corners. You can place a nightstand next to the bed. This arrangement creates two distinct zones for each occupant while allows enough free space in the centre of the room.

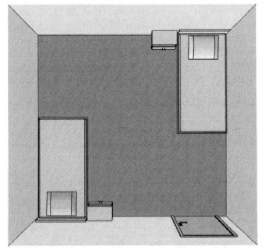

Headboards on opposite walls and in opposite corners.

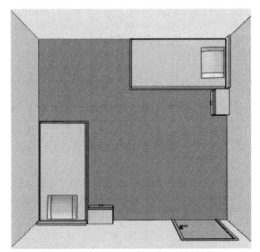

Headboards in opposite corners.

Double bed position in the bedroom

The double bed is placed against the center of the wall rather than the corner of the room, so as the long sides of the bed remain free. Otherwise, it is difficult for the sleepers to use the bed, lie or get out off it, while it is almost impossible to make the bed and clean the floor below. The double, queen-sized or king-sized bed can be placed:

Against the center of the wall with the headboard opposite the main door.

With this placement the headboard becomes the center of attention as someone enters the room.

Optimum double bed position. The headboard becomes the center of attention as somebody enters the room. Moreover, the sleepers feel more safe facing immediately the door without the need to reposition their body.

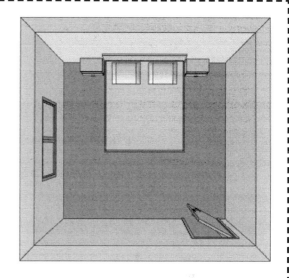

Second best choice for the double bed. Because of the window on the wall opposite the door, the bed is not placed on that wall. Generally, it is not reccomended to place the bed under a window, especially if the window opens frequently.

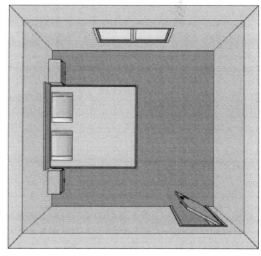

Against the center of a wall with the long side of the bed opposite the door.

Usually, this arrangement is selected only when the dimensions of the room do not allow the first two options.

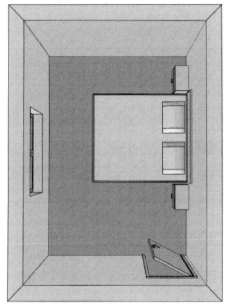

Due to the dimensions of the room and the position of the window, the bed was placed with the long side opposite the door. This arrangement seems imbalanced and might create a sense of uncertainty to the sleepers because the particular position does not provide a wide scope of the room. Generally, the larger the space in front of the bed the better the feeling while sleeping.

On a diagonal, in a corner of the room.

This is an inventive solution that unfortunatelly requires a lot of space. The bed is placed with the headboard against a corner of the room. In the empty corner behind the bed you can install a triangular built-in furniture, or you can place a plant or a floor lamp.

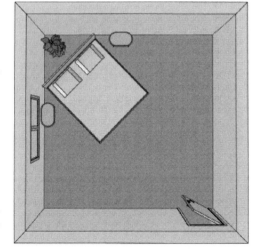

The bed is placed diagonally across the doorway. This placement provides the widest possible scope of the room while sleeping.

Types of bedrooms

To pick the right furniture and determine the proper room layout, you first need to know the different types of bedrooms. The type of bedroom and the location of the doors are a major factor in the overall bedroom design. Moreover, the bedroom layout and furniture selection depends highly on the room size.

A. Master bedroom

A master bedroom typically is the biggest bedroom in the house and it is meant for the parents. It may include additional spaces, accessible from the interior of the room, such as a walk-in closet and an adjoining bathroom. In this case the bedroom is called a master suite or an ensuite.

Functional zones in a master bedroom

The size of the bedroom defines how many functional zones can exist without being too multifunctional to disturb tranquil sleeping.

There can be the following functional zones in a master bedroom:
- Sleeping area
- Sitting area
- Reading area
- Correspondence desk area
- Kitchenette /coffee bar area
- Vanity makeup area

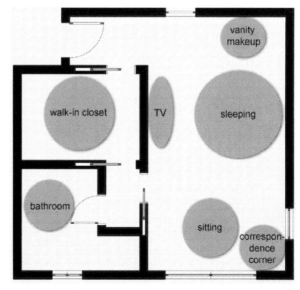

Case Study A

Case Study B

Master bedroom furniture

The most common pieces of furniture in a master bedroom are the following:
1. Double bed/ Queen size/ King bed size
2. Bedside tables
3. Vanity and stool
4. Desk with chairs
5. Chaise lounge/ Rocking seat
6. Coffee table
7. Ottomans or a bench
8. Flat TV
9. A set of armchairs
10. Kitchenette

You can certainly place other furniture like a dresser or a chest of drawers, a boudoir chair, a loveseat, a settee, etc

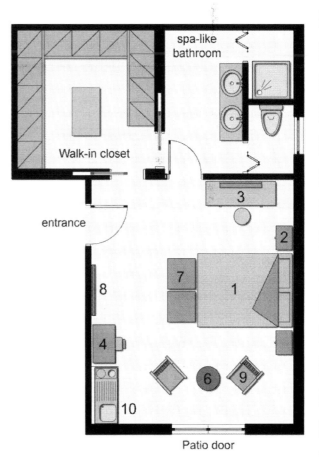

Master bedroom area

The bed is the focal point in any bedroom, as it is the dominant piece of furniture. The best place for the bed is against the longest wall, preferably opposite the entry door. Avoid placing the bed near the patio door or even under a window. You should ensure that there is enough space for bedside tables on either side of the bed. A streamlined bed arrangement is on a diagonal, providing there is plenty of space.

A bench or a pair of ottomans can be placed at the bed end. The ottomans can provide additional seating when moving to the other zones of the bedroom. A flat TV should be positioned so it can be seen from the bed. It can be placed on the wall above the dresser, but also in the sitting area. The computer desk, if there is any, should be placed away from the sleeping area.

A seating area is created with a pair of armchairs/ loveseats and a coffee table. Best location for a seating area, which constitutes a distinct functional zone, is by the window definitely away from the bed. If the size and layout of the bedroom allows, a space should be dedicated for a kitchenette/coffee bar. The unit can be placed either between the bedroom and the bath, into a nook, or even within the bathroom. The dresser is a storage place, and in most cases it can be placed on the left side of the bed. Alternatively, it can be placed anywhere in the bedroom, depending on the size and shape of the bedroom. A chest of drawers can also be placed anywhere in the bedroom. The vanity area can be positioned in a corner of the master bedroom or in the bathroom. The bathroom vanity includes one or two sinks on the countertop. Finally, you should consider the circulation paths in the room to avoid placing pieces of furniture in the way.

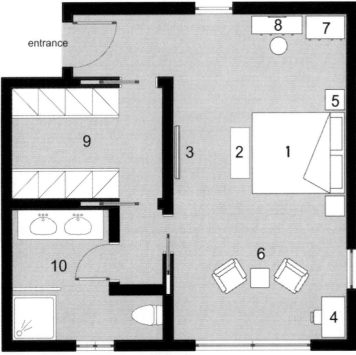

Master bedroom case study A   window

1. The bed is the focal point and it is placed opposite the entry door
2. At the bed end a bench is placed
3. A flat TV is positioned opposite the bed
4. The computer desk is placed in a corner away from the bed
5. Bedside tables are placed on either side of the bed
6. A pair of armchairs and a coffee table is placed by the window
7. A chest of drawers is placed in a corner of the bedroom
8. A vanity is placed next to the chest of drawers
9. Walk-in closet
10. Spa-like bathroom

Walk-in closet area

If the size of the master bedroom allows, a dual walk-in closet can be built. It should be near the bathroom for easy access. Preferably it should be located between the master bathroom and bedroom to allow an early riser taking a shower and getting dressed without disturbing the other person sleeping.

In the middle of the closet's dressing area a chair or an island unit with drawers can be placed, providing there is enough space. The closet can take many forms after having considered the space available and the storage needed (lineal feet/meters of rod, shelves and drawers).

Spa-like bathroom area

The bathroom space has also functional zones, such as a toilet area, a bathing area and a sink area. All areas should be organized in a manner to let the two users utilize different areas within the bathroom concurrently.

A long vanity with two sinks can be placed to allow the couple to do their morning routines at the same time. The W.C. should ensure privacy by being installed in a separate space.

Regarding the shower options two solutions can be selected: a bathtub accommodating two people and a shower enclosure.

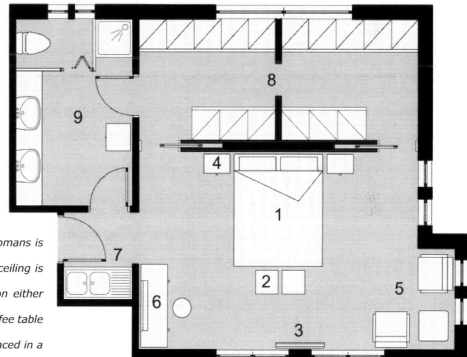

Master bedroom case study B

1. The bed is the focal point
2. At the bed end a pair of ottomans is placed
3. A flat TV hanging from the ceiling is arranged opposite the bed
4. Bedside tables are placed on either side of the bed
5. A pair of armchairs and a coffee table are placed by the window
6. A dresser with a mirror is placed in a corner of the room
7. A kitchenette is placed into a nook at the entrance of the room
8. Dual walk-in next to the master bedroom
9. Spa-like master bathroom

B. Double bedroom

A double is a bedroom for two people or a couple who share a double bed or two single beds. A double bedroom is usually smaller than a master bedroom without the amenities of the master bedroom.

Functional zones in a double bedroom

A double bedroom serves multiple purposes, such as sleeping, dressing, reading, etc. Different activities in the room should be considered for the definition of functional zones accordingly. There can be the following functional zones in a double bedroom:
-Sleeping/watching TV area
-Sitting/reading area
-Storage area
-Vanity makeup area

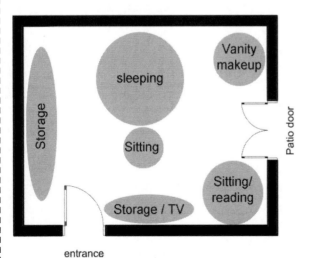

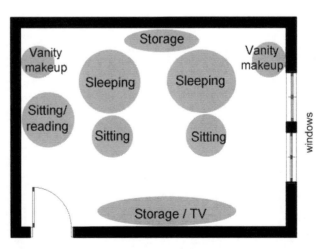

Double bedroom furniture and layouts

The bed should be the focal point of the room. The best arrangement for the bed is in the center of the room's most visible wall, which is usually opposite the entry door. The bed should be flanked by two small-scale dressers used as bedside tables.

The wardrobe, one of the largest pieces of furniture, is considered to be the second most important furniture item in a bedroom. There are many options available in selecting a wardrobe, such as built-in wardrobes, free standing wardrobes, fitted wardrobes, open hanging wardrobes which all meet storage purposes. The size and shape of the wardrobe and also the wardrobe's position in a bedroom depend on the size and shape of the bedroom. It can be placed against a wall on one side of the bed, ensuring that the bed is not within the arc of opening wardrobe doors and drawers. It can also be placed opposite the bed, leaving free space as previously mentioned, next to a wall mounted flat screen TV.

Alternatively, a pier group bed can be selected. A bench or a pair of ottomans at the foot of the bed provide a sitting area in the bedroom. A small-size armchair or a rocking chair in a corner serves the same purpose. A makeup vanity with a mirror above and a matching chair can be positioned anywhere in the bedroom.

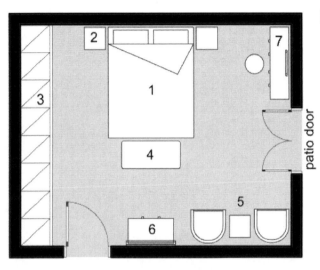

Double bedroom furniture & layouts

1. Double bed. *The bed is placed in the center of the wall opposite the entry door.*
2. Bedside tables. *Two small scale dressers are used as bedside tables.*
3. Built-in wardrobe.
4. Bench. *A bench is placed at the foot of the bed.*
5. A pair of armchairs and coffee table *provide a sitting area*
6. Dresser.
7. Vanity and stool. *The makeup vanity is placed in the corner of the room.*

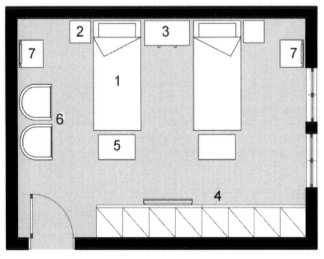

1. Single beds. *Two single beds are placed in the center of the wall opposite the entry door.*
2. Bedside tables. *Two small scale dressers are used as bedside tables.*
3. Chest of drawers. *A chest of drawers between the beds provides privacy.*
4. Wardrobe. *A wardrobe with TV space is placed opposite the bed.*
5. Bench. *A small bench is placed at the foot of each single bed.*
6. Armchairs. *A pair of armchairs on one side of the bed provides a sitting area*
7. Makeup vanities. *Two small makeup vanities are placed on one side of each single bed*

Double bedroom furniture & layouts

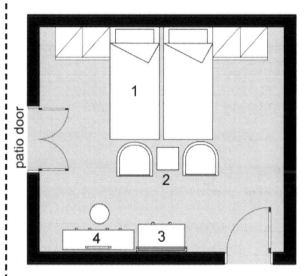

1. Single beds. *The beds are placed next to each other in the center of the wall opposite the entry door.*
2. Armchair. *A pair of armchairs at the foot of the bed provides a sitting area.*
3. Dresser. *A flat TV is placed above the dresser.*
4. Vanity and stool.

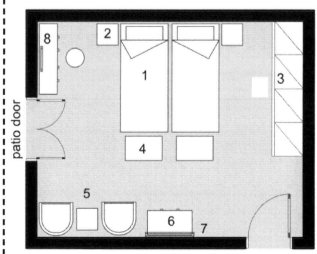

1. Single beds. *Two single beds are placed in the center of the wall opposite the entry door.*
2. Bedside tables. *Two small scale dressers are used as bedside tables.*
3. Wardrobe. *A free standing wardrobe is placed against the wall on one side of the bed.*
4. Ottomans. *A pair of ottomans is placed at the foot of the bed.*
5. A pair of armchairs and coffee table *provide a sitting area.*
6. Dresser.
7. TV. *The flat TV is placed above the dresser opposite the bed*
8. Vanity and stool. *The makeup vanity is placed in the corner of the room.*

Children's bedroom

A children's bedroom is usually smaller than the master bedroom. It is more than just a place for sleeping. It can be considered as a multipurpose space to do the homework, listen to music, read, store the toys, play games with friends etc. A children's bedroom can be classified according to the age of the child as follows:

C. Nursery room (baby's bedroom)

A nursery room is used to accommodate children during their infancy and toddler hood (0-36 months)

Safety is the primary consideration when designing the nursery. Another option that should also be considered is its ability to be converted into a child's room. This means that the nursery furniture should be convertible and combinable with new pieces to update the look of the room. For example, convertible cribs can be transformed into toddler beds, changing tables can be converted into dressers, etc.

Functional zones in a nursery

Considering that a baby's needs are quite simple, such as sleep, food, clean diapers, dress and love, certain functional zones should be defined.

-Sleeping area
-Feeding area
-Changing area

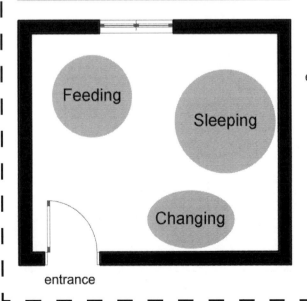

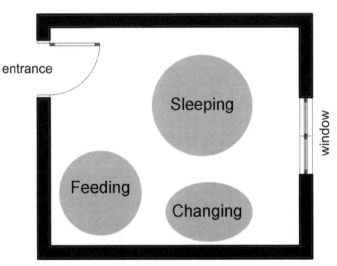

Nursery furniture

The most common pieces of furniture in a nursery room are the following:

1. Crib with mattress
1a. Cradle/Bassinet/Co-sleeper (suitable for the baby's first 4 months)
2. Changing table
3. Baby's dresser
4. Bedside table
5. Glider/ Rocker

You can certainly place other furniture, such as a baby park or a travel bed

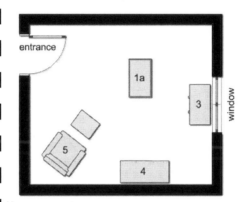 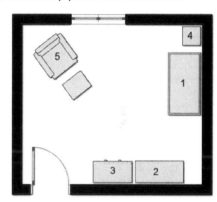

Nursery room layout

The crib is the focal point in any nursery. A standard placement is against an interior wall near the door, so that it is visible while entering the room. This location ensures that the baby will have a warmer and quieter sleep.

The crib should be placed away from windows to ensure that the baby is warm and safe from reaching the curtains or window blinds.

The changing table should be positioned close to the crib for carrying the baby to be cleaned more easily. The rocking chair/glider can be placed near the window, so the mother can look outside while sitting, feeding or cradling the baby. The baby dresser should be placed near the changing table. The bedside table should be placed away from the crib, so that the baby can't reach it once crawling and standing.

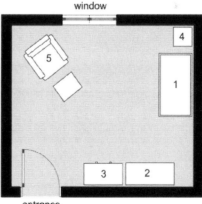

1. The crib is the focal point of the nursery. It is placed in the middle of the room.
2. The changing table is placed close to the crib.
3. The baby dresser is placed next to the changing table.
4. The bedside table is placed in a corner.
5. The rocking chair/glider is placed near the window.

D. Kids's bedroom

A kid's room is used to accommodate small children during their childhood (4-12 years). Furniture should be chosen depending on the number of the children and their age. The size of the room is also essential. Safety is again the primary consideration in the room layout.

Functional zones in a kid's bedroom

For a child, a bedroom is not only a space for sleeping. It is a place to do various activities, such as sleeping, doing homework, playing games, listening to music, chatting with friends, storing numerous belongings and doing hobbies. All these activities define two functional zones in a child's bedroom.

1. Rest/sleeping zone
2. Playing zone (including work and study area)

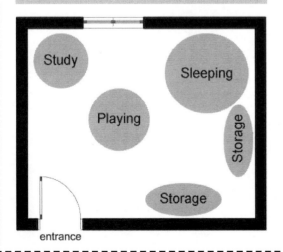

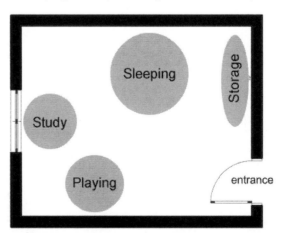

158

Kid's bedroom furniture and layouts

When two children share the same bedroom, beds are arranged in different combinations depending on the shape and size of the room. Furniture should be arranged to provide open space for play. Toys storage units should be located in the play zone away from the bed for safety reasons. The bed should not be positioned close to the window so that the child does not wake up early in the morning.

If there is adequate space, a table and a chair can be placed away from the sleeping zone. The main pieces of furniture (bed, wardrobe, bookcase, etc) should be placed against walls for spaciousness and safety reasons. The desk should be placed in the study area. A nightstand should be placed next to the bed to support a night lamp, a clock, a glass of water, etc.

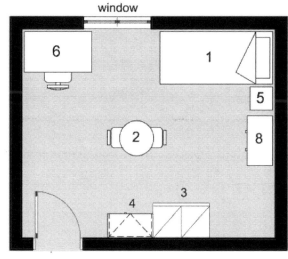

All pieces of furniture are arranged to provide open space for play. The main pieces of furniture are arranged against the walls for spaciousness.
1. Bed/ Bunk. *The bed is positioned away from the window.*
2. A table with chairs *is placed is the playing zone.*
3. Freestanding wardrobe.
4. Bookcase.
5. Bedside table.
6. Desk with chair. *The desk is placed in the study area away from the bed.*

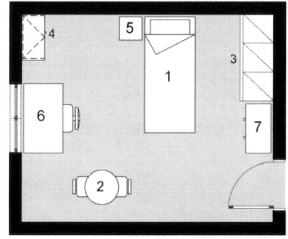

All pieces of furniture are arranged to provide open space for play. The main pieces of furniture are arranged against the walls for spaciousness.
1. Bed/ Bunk. *The placement of the headboard against the wall allows free space for play..*
2. A table with chairs *is placed is the playing zone.*
3. Freestanding wardrobe.
4. Bookcase.
5. Bedside table.
6. Desk with chair. *The desk is placed in the study area away from the bed.*
7. Dresser. *A dresser is positioned near the bedside table.*

E. Teen's bedroom

A teen's room is used to accommodate children during their teenage years (13-18 years). When it comes to the layout of a teenager's bedroom, certain options should be considered, such as a study area, a storage area and an open space for socializing. Accommodating two teenagers in the same bedroom today is less common than it used to be and arises problems, such as privacy and extra space to fit in the absolute necessary furniture.

Functional zones in a teen's bedroom

As children grow to become teenagers, their interests differ from childhood. They often desire a furniture arrangement that suits their new needs and interests. Consequently, existing functional zones should be redefined.

-Sleeping zone
-Study zone
-Lounge zone
-Storage zone

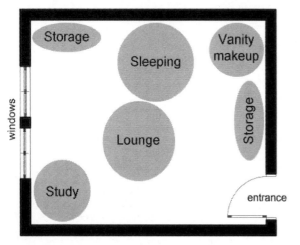

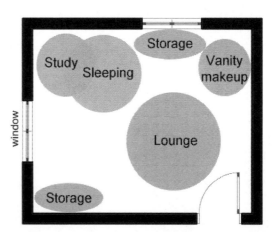

Teen's bedroom furniture and layouts

The day bed should be placed against a wall, so that there is free space left for activities. An extra bed can be stored underneath the bed and pulled out for hosting overnight friends. If a loft bed is selected, the study area can be placed under it.

A funky night stand should be positioned near the bed. The dresser or the wardrobe can be placed against a wall or in the middle of the room creating two distinct functional areas on each side, providing the room is spacious enough. Additional storage space should be found to meet the needs of the teenager in almost all pieces of furniture.

A distinct study zone can be created by placing an L-shaped desk into a corner with the matching chair. Adjacent to the desk a bookcase or a shelving system can be positioned. The lounge area is defined by the available free space of the room.

A click-clack sofa or flip-top ottomans can create a leisure space in the bedroom. Small lounge area can be created by tossing bean bag chairs in the center of the room surrounding a small accent table.

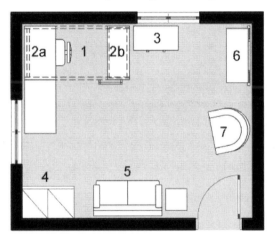

1. The **loft bed** ensures the study area under it.
2. The **study area** includes the desk (2a) and the bookcase (2b).
3. The **dresser** is placed under the window or against a wall.
4. The **wardrobe** is placed against a wall.
5. A **click-clack sofa** provides sitting area.
6. A **vanity mirror** is placed in a corner of the room.
7. **Bean bag chair.**

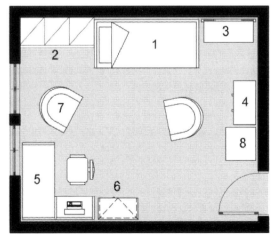

1. The **day bed** is placed against a wall to leave free space for activities.
2. The **wardrobe** is placed against a wall.
3. A **vanity mirror** is placed in a corner of the room.
4. The **dresser** is placed against a wall.
5. A **L-shaped desk** is placed into a corner with a matching chair.
6. A **bookcase** is placed adjacent to the desk.
7. **Bean bag chairs** are tossed in the center of the room.
8. A **flip-top ottoman** provides storage and sitting area as well.

Shared bedrooms layouts for kids and teens

Two twin beds can be arranged in various ways, which ensure providing space to both occupants. A standard placement is the two beds to be located next to each other making a larger bed, especially useful for smaller rooms. The head to head placement creates an L-shape bed layout in a corner of the room. The footboard to footboard placement is suitable for oblong bedrooms. The beds are placed against a long wall with footboards facing each other. Alternatively, nightstands can be placed between the footboards.

The placement of headboards against the same wall with a piece of furniture between them ensures privacy for each occupant. The bunk/loft beds placement also ensures privacy, especially between children of the opposite sex. Moreover, this placement provides free space in a small bedroom for other furniture to be arranged and also for the children's various activities. If vacant place still exists, additional pieces of furniture can be placed, such as a reading nook, extra storage units, etc.

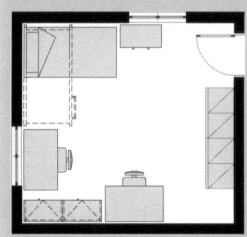

The bunk/loft bed placement ensures privacy, especially between children of the opposite sex.

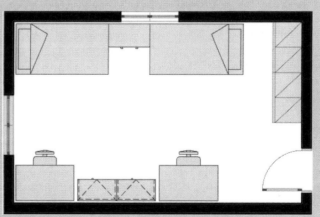

The footboard to footboard placement is suitable for oblong bedrooms.

Different furniture layouts varying according to the child's age

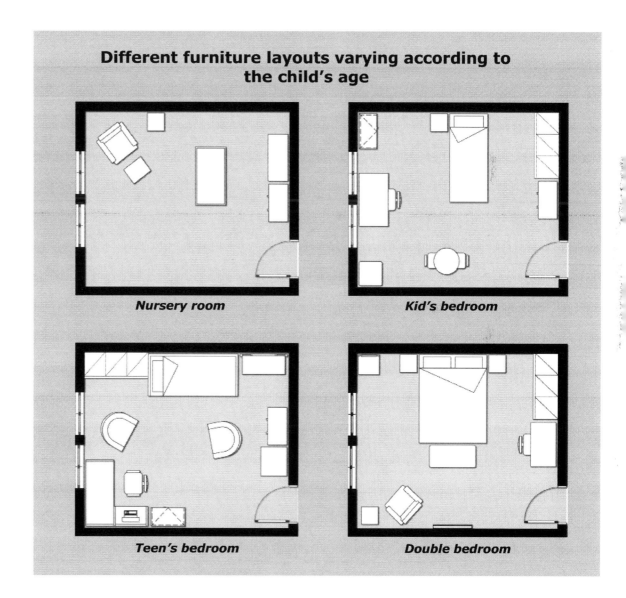

Nursery room

Kid's bedroom

Teen's bedroom

Double bedroom

F. Guest room

Some houses have a spare room for hosting guests. A guest room often has an adjacent bathroom to enhance guests' privacy, which is most appreciated by the guests.

Functional zones in a guest-double bedroom

A guest room is mainly used to host guests and it should be restful and welcoming. Functional zones in a guest room
1. Sleeping/watching TV area
2. Reading area
3. Storage area
4. Vanity makeup area

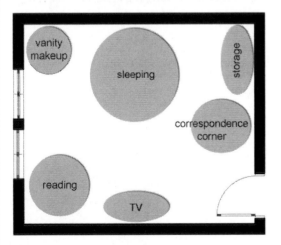

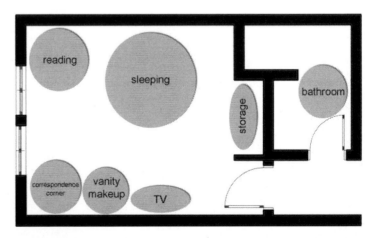

Guest's room furniture

The most common pieces of furniture in a guest room are the following:
1. Double bed
2. Bedside tables
3. Wardrobe dresser combo
4. Bench
5. Vanity and stool
6. Lounge chair and table
7. Writing table
8. Flat TV

Guest room layouts

As the main purpose of a guest room is providing a welcoming feel, the bed should be the focal point. It should be positioned in the middle of the wall opposite the entrance. Two bedside tables on each side of the bed are quite necessary. A wardrobe dresser combo should be placed against a wall. A bench should be placed at the end of the bed to provide a place to sit or to put a suitcase for packing and unpacking.

A small bedroom vanity can be placed in a corner of the room. In the opposite corner, a reading nook can be created with a lounge chair and an end table.

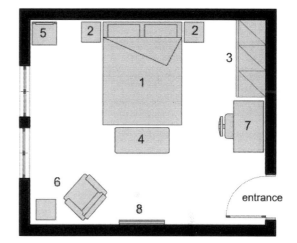

1. The bed is positioned in the middle of the wall opposite the entrance
2. Two bedside tables are placed on each side of the bed
3. A wardrobe dresser combo is placed against a wall
4. A bench is arranged at the end of the bed
5. A small bedroom vanity is placed in a corner of the room
6. In the opposite corner, a lounge chair and an end table are placed
7. A writing table is placed against a wall
8. A wall mounted flat TV is placed opposite the bed
9. Adjacent bathroom

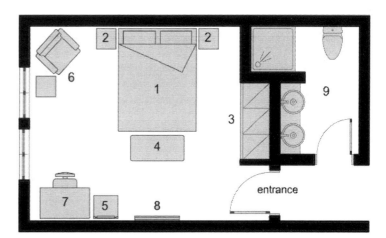

Bedroom layouts with one bed

Below, some typical bedroom layouts with their measurements, both in metric and imperial system are presented. Most of them combine practicality and proper use of space.

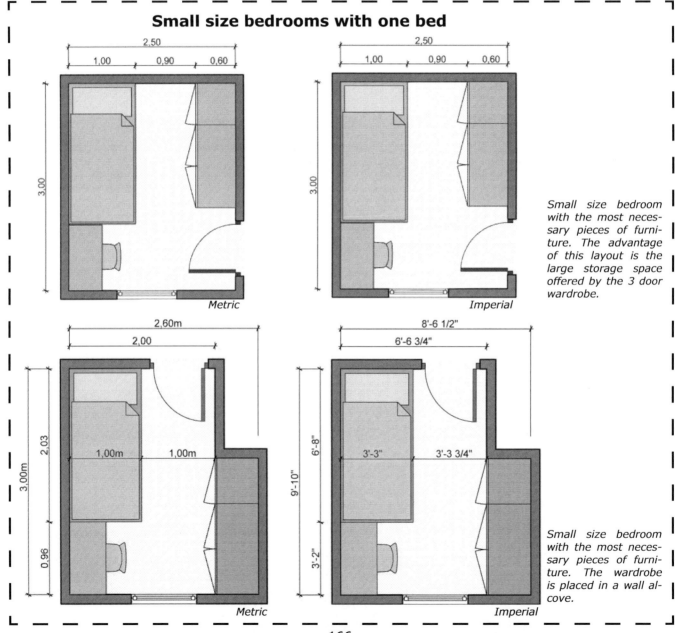

Small size bedrooms with one bed

Metric

Imperial

Small size bedroom with the most necessary pieces of furniture. The advantage of this layout is the large storage space offered by the 3 door wardrobe.

Metric

Imperial

Small size bedroom with the most necessary pieces of furniture. The wardrobe is placed in a wall alcove.

Small size bedrooms with one bed

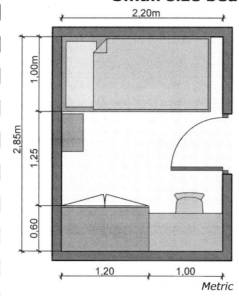

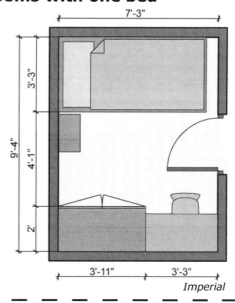

2.20m

1.00m

2.85m

1.25

0.60

1.20   1.00

Metric

7'-3"

3'-3"

9'-4"

4'-1"

2'

3'-11"   3'-3"

Imperial

Small size bedroom. Next to the bed a nightstand can be placed.

Long and narrow bedrooms with one bed

Usually, long and narrow rooms are difficult to arrange and furnish. However, the arrangement of a kid's bedroom with one bed is easy by positioning the bed with its long side against the wall.

The benefit of this arrangement is the placement of the desk under the window and the additional placement of a bookcase.

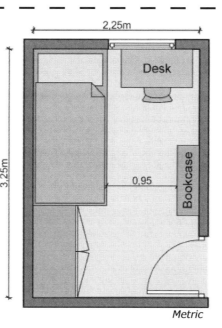

2.25m

3.25m

0.95

Desk

Bookcase

Metric

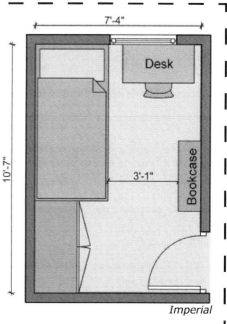

7'-4"

10'-7"

3'-1"

Desk

Bookcase

Imperial

Long and narrow bedrooms with one bed

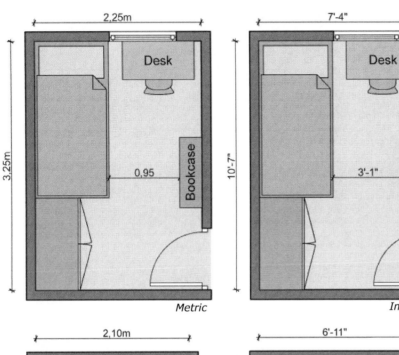

Metric   Imperial

A long bedroom. The bed is placed in the middle of the long wall leaving at the end of the room, enough space for a desk and a wardrobe.

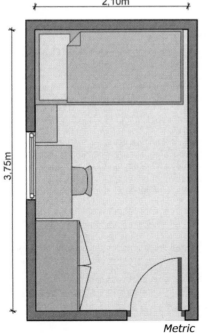 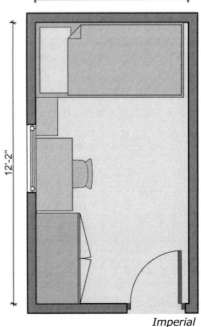

Metric   Imperial

The bed is placed at the end of the room with a nightstand beside the bed. On the empty wall you can place a bookcase or apply wallpaper.

Medium size bedrooms with one bed

In medium size bedrooms you can position the single bed with the headboard against the wall and a bedside table next to it. Moreover, you can create diferent functional zones, such as a play zone or a seating area, arranging relevevant pieces of furniture like armchairs, loveseats, dressers, small tables, etc.

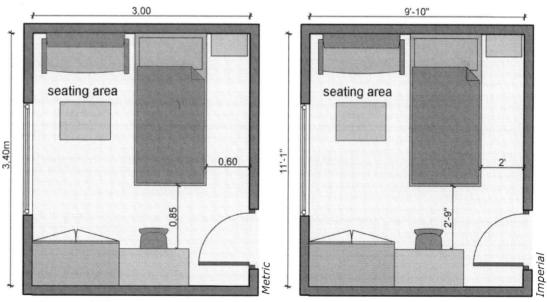

Medium size bedroom. By adding a loveaseat or a sofa bed you can create a seating area.

Medium size bedrooms with one bed

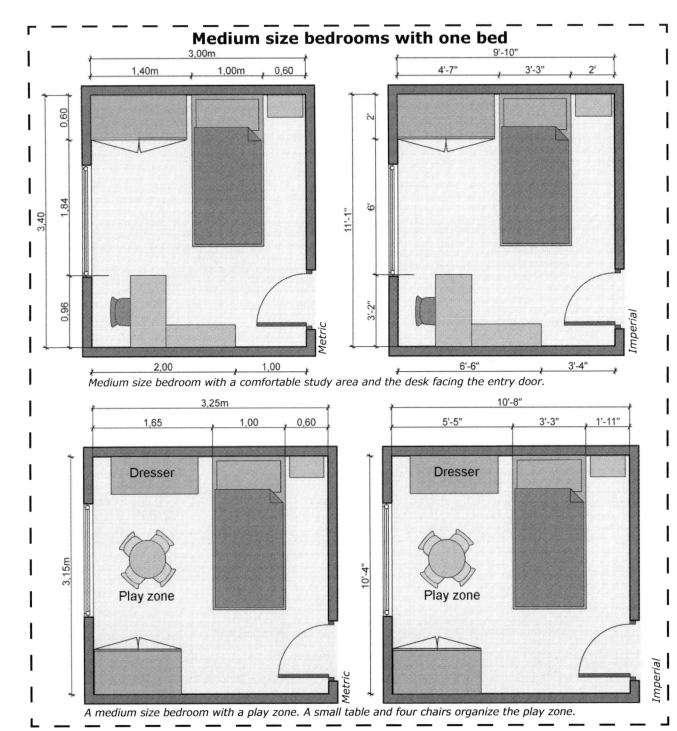

Medium size bedroom with a comfortable study area and the desk facing the entry door.

A medium size bedroom with a play zone. A small table and four chairs organize the play zone.

Medium size bedrooms with one bed

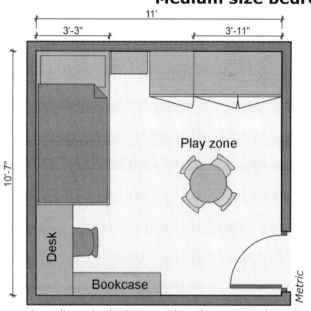

A medium size bedroom with a play zone, a three door wardrobe and a comfortable study area.

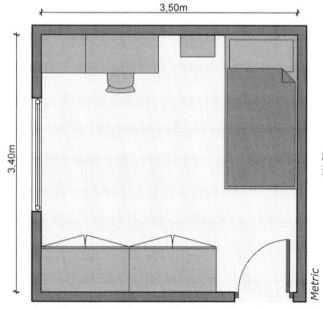

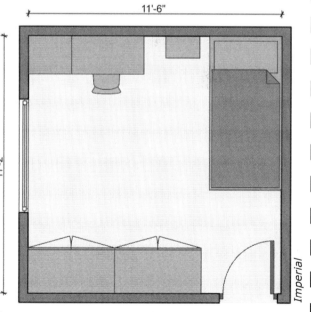

A medium size bedroom with a large, four door wardrobe.

Large size bedrooms with one bed

In large size bedrooms with one bed the available space is more than enough to fit everything you imagine, such as a large storage wardrobe, a dresser, a desk, etc. Moreover, you can create distinct study area, play zone or even a conversation area.

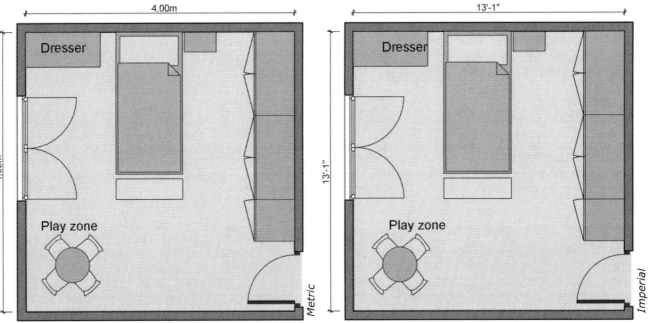

A large size bedroom with a five door wardrobe, play zone and plenty of free space.

Large size bedrooms with one bed

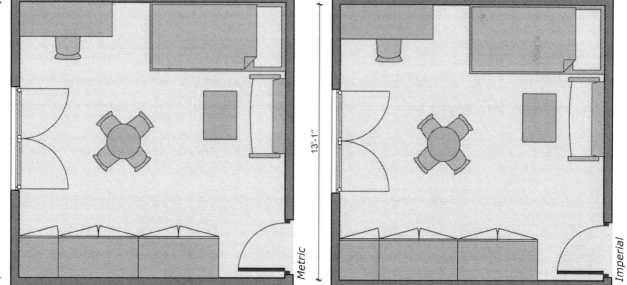

4,00m   13'-1"

Dresser

4,00   13'-1"

Desk   Desk

Metric   Imperial

A large size bedroom with a five door wardrobe and a comfortable study area.

4,00m   13'-1"

4,00   13'-1"

Metric   Imperial

The bed is placed with the headborad in one corner of the room. Inevitably, enough free space is left for placing a large wardrobe and a sofa.

Bedroom layouts with two twin beds

In case there is a need for two people (children/teens/guests) to coexist in a bedroom, you should consider various placements of the two twin beds you need to fit in this space. Below, some typical bedroom layouts with their measurements, both in metric and imperial system are presented. Most of them combine practicality and proper use of space.

Small size 2 twins bedrooms

When the available space is small, you should only arrange the absolute necessary furniture, such as a bedside table/dresser, a wardrobe and a desk with a chair. The location of the entry door and the window/patio door and the proportions of the space provide more restrictions when it comes to organizing the room.

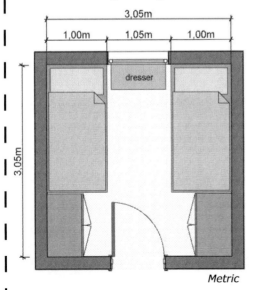

Metric

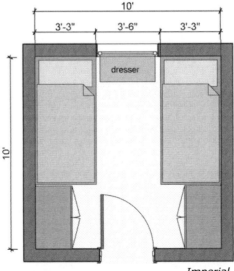

Imperial

The drawback of this arrangement is that due to the lack of space you have to choose placing either two freestanding wardrobes at either side of the entry door or a wardrobe at one side and a desk with a chair at the other. You can also place a dresser between the twin beds instead of a shared bedside table.

174

Small size 2 twins bedrooms

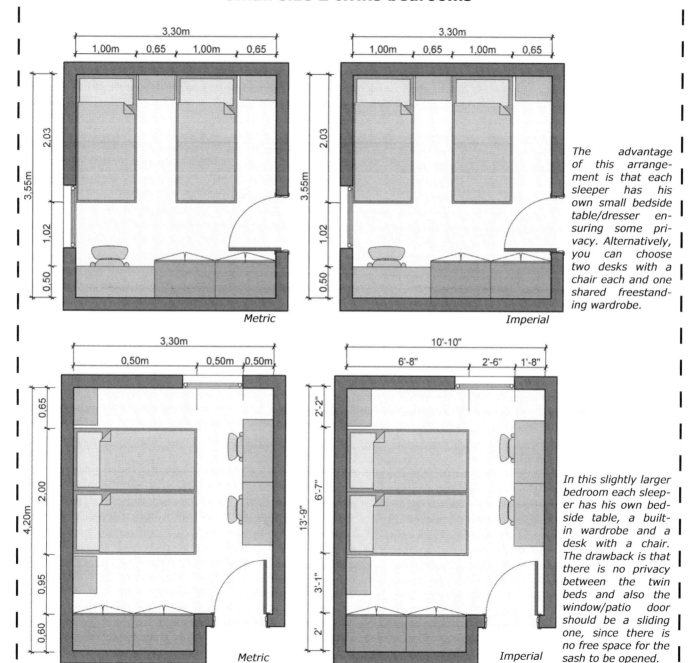

The advantage of this arrangement is that each sleeper has his own small bedside table/dresser ensuring some privacy. Alternatively, you can choose two desks with a chair each and one shared freestanding wardrobe.

Metric

Imperial

In this slightly larger bedroom each sleeper has his own bedside table, a built-in wardrobe and a desk with a chair. The drawback is that there is no privacy between the twin beds and also the window/patio door should be a sliding one, since there is no free space for the sash to be opened.

Metric

Imperial

Medium size 2 twins bedrooms

In medium size bedrooms with two twin beds there is enough space available for more functional zones, such as a play zone. Alternatively, you can create individual study areas with a bookcase for each occupant.

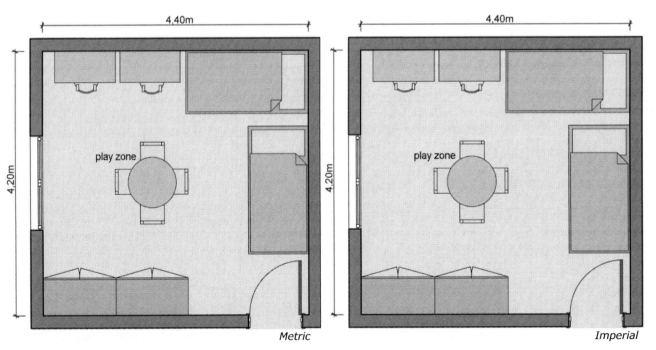

Metric

Imperial

By placing two twin beds in a corner to form an L-shaped arrangement, free space is allowed at the center of the room in which you can create a play zone.

Medium size 2 twins bedrooms

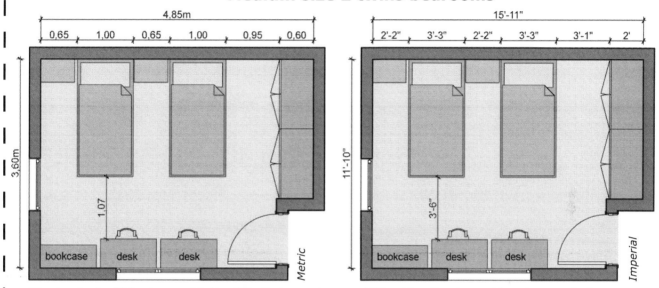

The drawback of this placement is the difficulty in creating an additional functional zone. The advantage is the privacy of each sleeper.

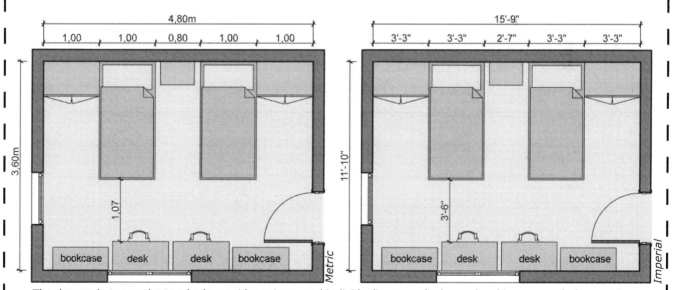

The dresser between the two beds provides privacy and individuality as each sleeper has his own wardrobe next to their bed.

Narrow 2 twins bedrooms

Narrow bedrooms need to be arranged in a way so that they can look wider and balanced. Their awkward shape may make the functionality troublesome.

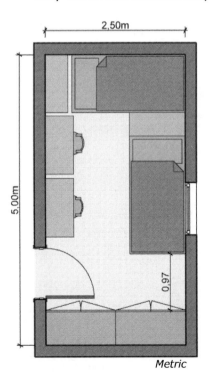

Metric

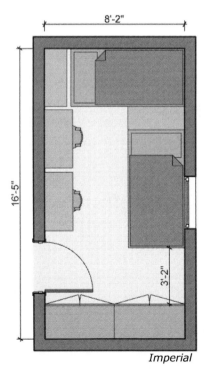

Imperial

By arranging a sleeping corner (beds on an angle) and the storage area (wardrobes) at the narrow ends, the bedroom looks wider and less space is wasted.

Narrow 2 twins bedrooms

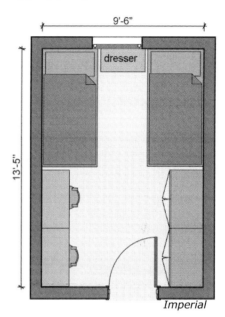

2,90m

4,10m

dresser

Metric

9'-6"

13'-5"

dresser

Imperial

The beds are placed symmetrically along the long axis of the room taking advantage of the location of the entry door and the window in the middle of the room.

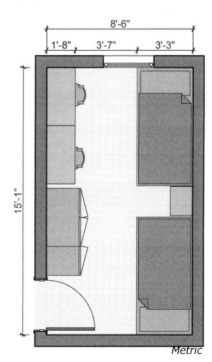

8'-6"

1'-8" 3'-7" 3'-3"

15'-1"

Metric

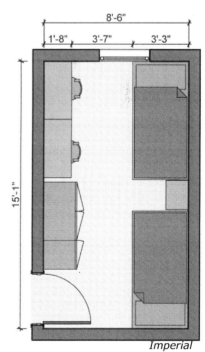

8'-6"

1'-8" 3'-7" 3'-3"

15'-1"

Imperial

Two zones are arranged against the long walls; the sleeping zone is placed opposite the entry door. The study and storage zone are arranged opposite the sleeping area and free space is left in the middle of the room.

Large size 2 twins bedrooms

The roomier large bedrooms can accommodate more pieces of furniture in different functional zones, such as extra storage, a sofa with a table, a dresser etc. Each sleeper can have his own bedside table, bookcase and desk with a chair.

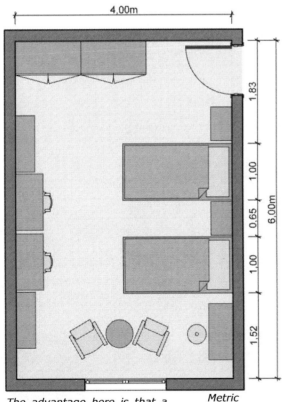

The advantage here is that a living/play zone is organized near the window.

Metric

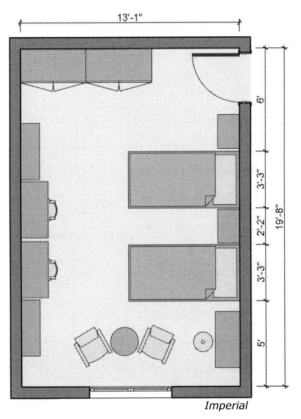

Imperial

Large size 2 twins bedrooms

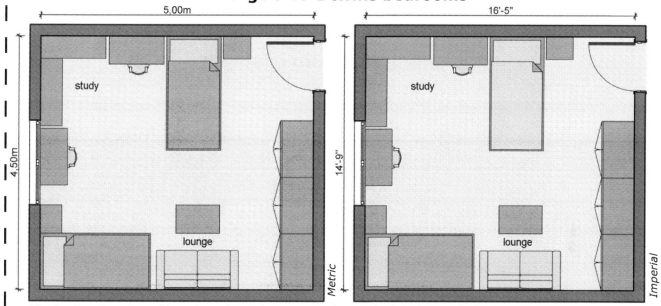

The furniture layout provides privacy for each occupant. The drawback is that one bed is located near the entry door.

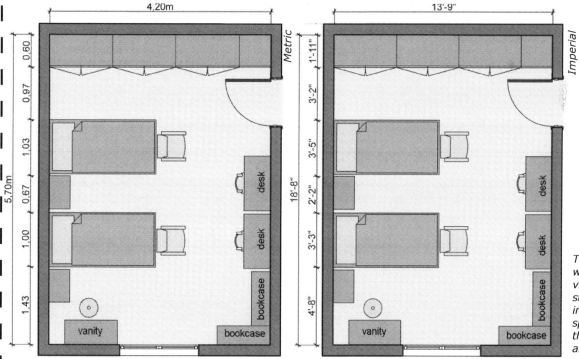

The built-in wardrobe provides extra storage and improves the space usage in this bedroom arrangement.

Double Bedroom layouts

Small size double bedrooms

The double bed is the focal point of any room and it is usually placed opposite the door. In small bedrooms placement options are very limited as there should be enough space left at either side of the bed so as it can be accessed comfortably.

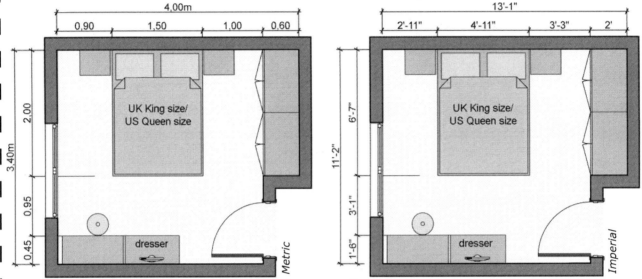

The built-in wardrobe creates a sense of spaciousness as its position is very discrete. Thus, opposite the bed a vanity and a dresser with a TV set can be placed.

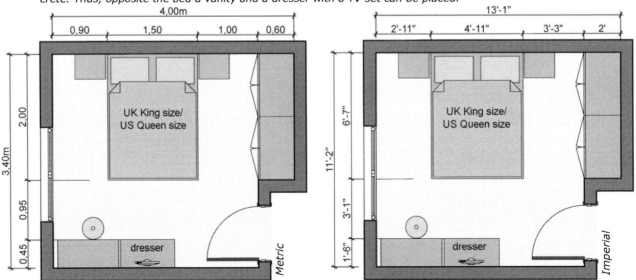

The drawback in this arrangement is that there is no space for a dresser. Moreover, the TV set should be integrated in the built-in wardrobe.

Medium size double bedrooms

Medium size double bedrooms are more flexible when it comes to furniture placement. Additionally furniture of larger size can be arranged in the room and more functional zones can be created.

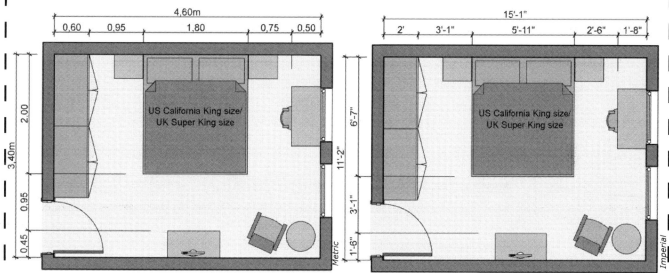

Although there is more than one functional zone, there is enough space to move easily around the bed.

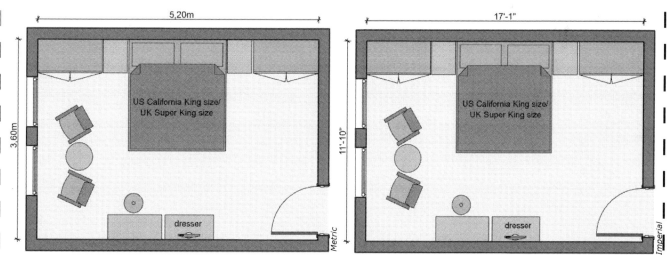

The double bed is flanked by a construction with two wardrobes and bedside tables integrated. This placement makes the room look spacious.

Large size double bedrooms

Arranging furniture in a large bedroom is a very pleasant challenge as there's plenty of space available. In large bedrooms furniture should be placed in a way that the room doesn't look either overcrowded or empty.

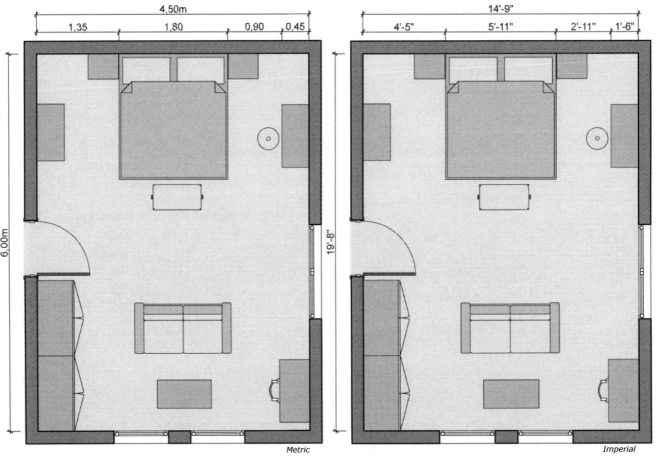

The location of the entry door divides the space into two areas with various functional zones.

Large size double bedrooms

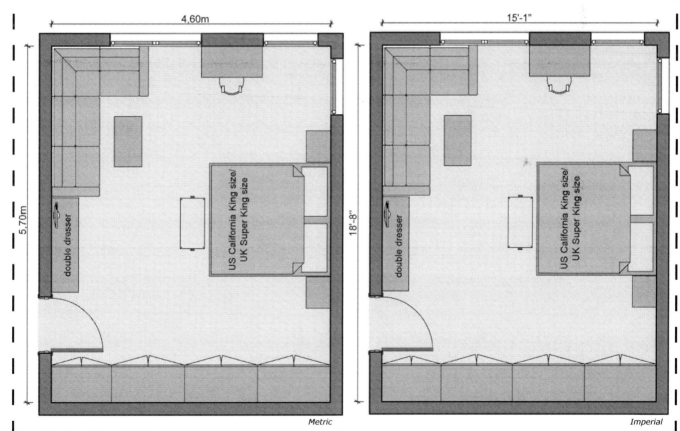

4.60m

5.70m

double dresser

US California King size/
UK Super King size

Metric

15'-1"

18'-8"

double dresser

US California King size/
UK Super King size

Imperial

The advantage of this placement is the large storage area.

I. FURNITURE CUTOUTS

Appendix I: Furniture cutouts

The reader is cautioned that furniture measurements vary form supplier to supplier and from source to source. Although every effort has been made to ensure that the information is correct, the reader is cautioned to consult the manufacturers of items for specific dimension data.

Although every effort has been made to present accurate information the authors assume no liability or responsibility for damage to persons or property alleged to have occurred as a direct or indirect consequence of the use and application of any of the contents of this book.

The furniture symbols are in scale. So, in case you print them do not enlarge or reduce the pages. Simply photocopy them keeping the scale same.

ARMCHAIRS

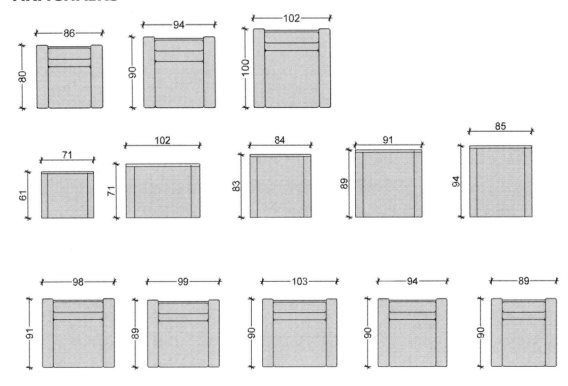

CHAIRS

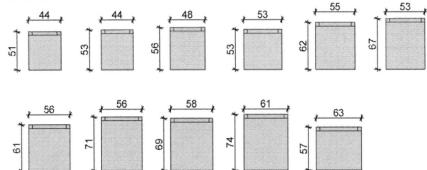

METRIC / SCALE 1:50 / measurments in cm

ARMCHAIRS

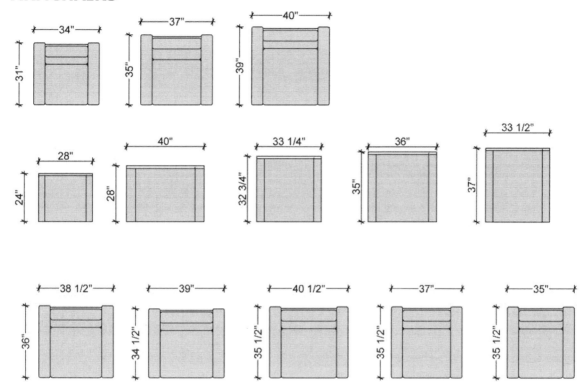

CHAIRS

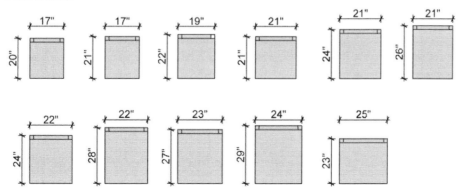

IMPERIAL / SCALE 1/4"= 1'-0"/ measurements in inches

LOVESEATS- TWO SEATER SOFAS

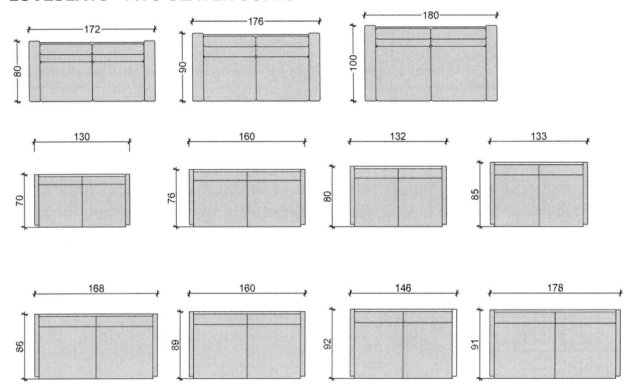

LOVESEATS- TWO SEATER SOFAS

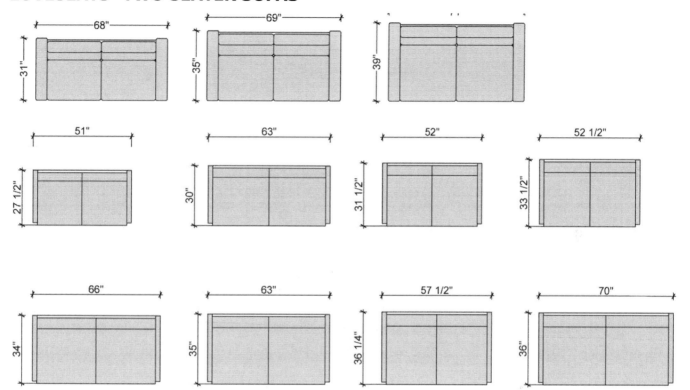

THREE SEATER SOFAS

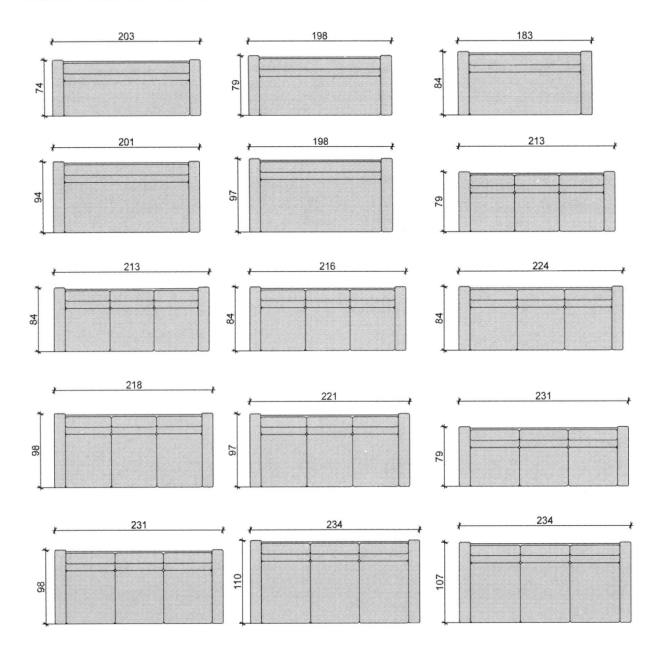

METRIC / SCALE 1:50 / measurments in cm

THREE SEATER SOFAS

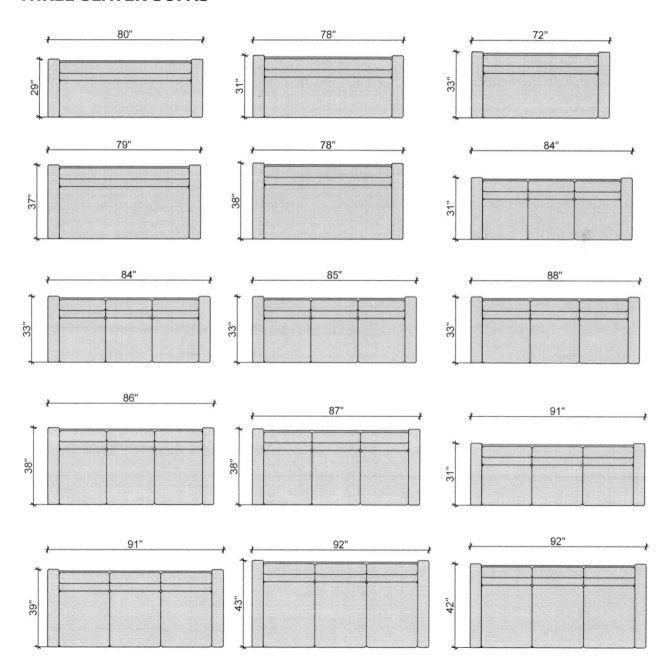

IMPERIAL / SCALE 1/4"= 1'-0"/ measurements in inches

CHAISE LONGUES

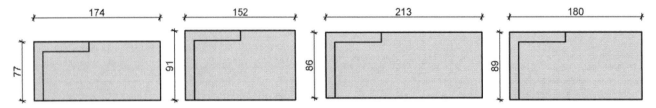

SOFA-BEDS

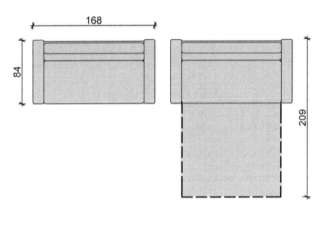

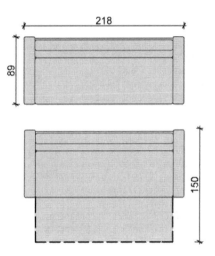

FUTONS

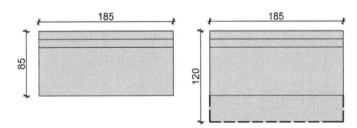

METRIC / SCALE 1:50 / measurments in cm

CHAISE LONGUES

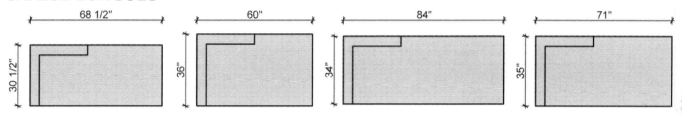

SOFA-BEDS

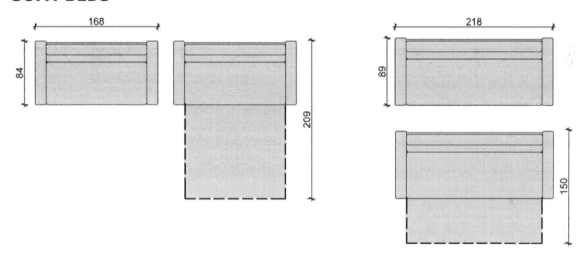

FUTONS

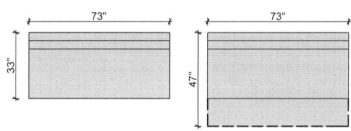

IMPERIAL / SCALE 1/4"= 1'-0"/ measurements in inches

BEAN BAGS

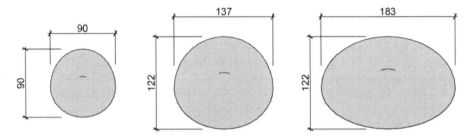

OTTOMANS

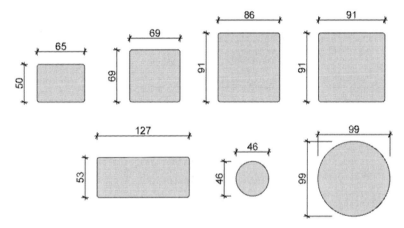

BEAN BAGS

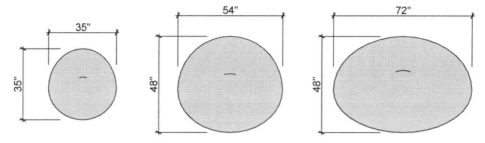

OTTOMANS

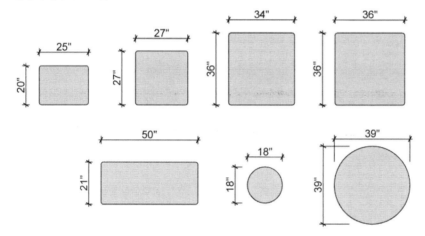

IMPERIAL / SCALE 1/4"= 1'-0"/ measurements in inches

SECTIONALS TYPE A

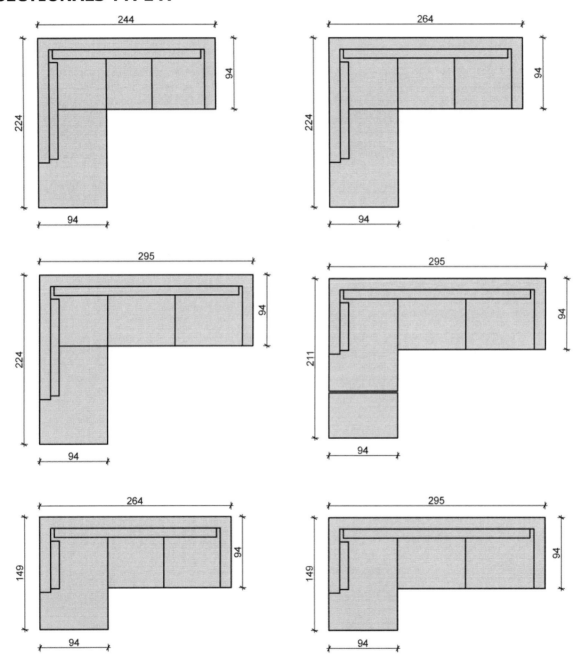

METRIC / SCALE 1:50 / measurments in cm

SECTIONALS TYPE A

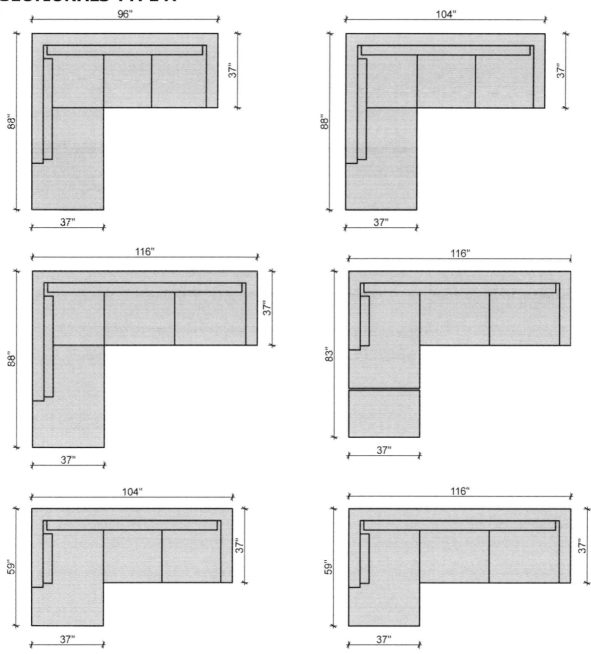

IMPERIAL / SCALE 1/4''= 1'-0''/ measurements in inches

SECTIONALS TYPE B

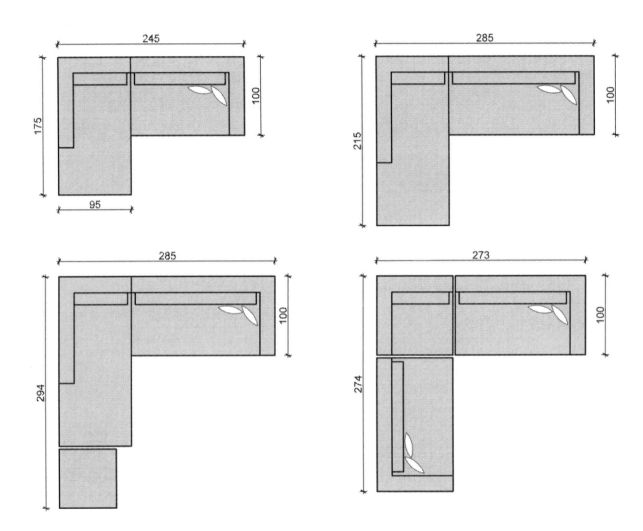

METRIC / SCALE 1:50 / measurments in cm

SECTIONALS TYPE B

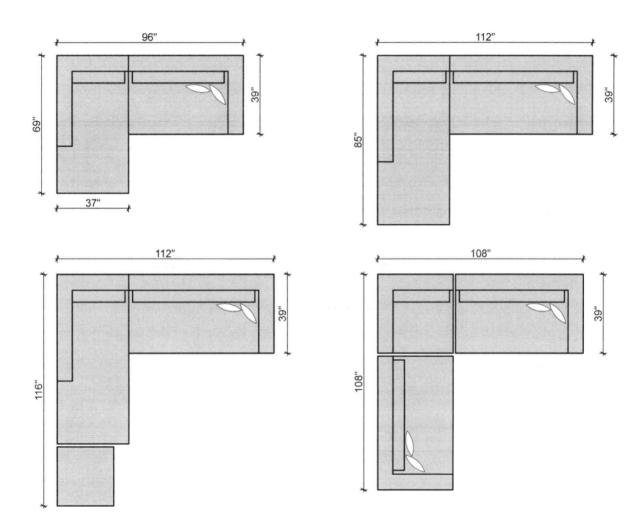

IMPERIAL / SCALE 1/4"= 1'-0"/ measurements in inches

SECTIONALS TYPE B

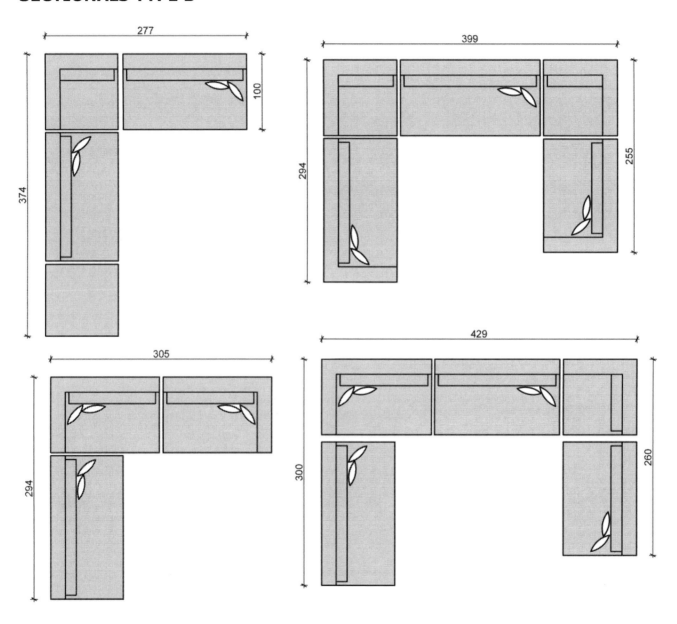

METRIC / SCALE 1:50 / measurments in cm

SECTIONALS TYPE B

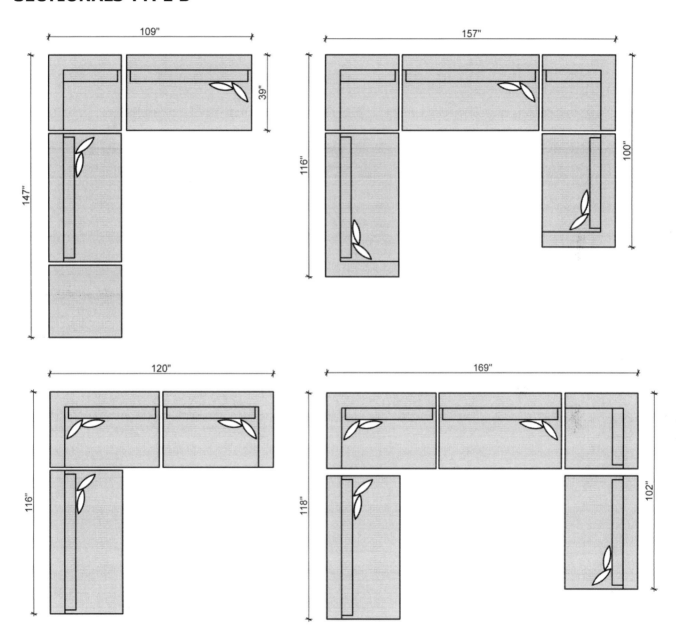

IMPERIAL / SCALE 1/4''= 1'-0''/ measurements in inches

COFFEE TABLES

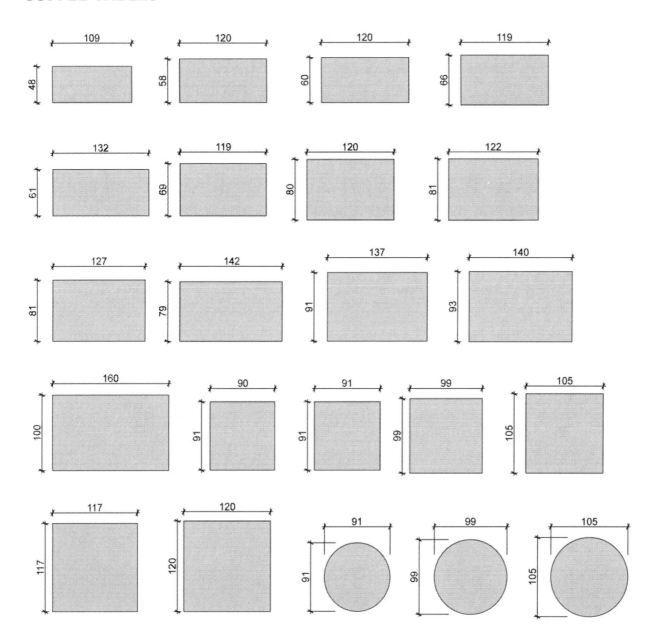

METRIC / SCALE 1:50 / measurments in cm

COFFEE TABLES

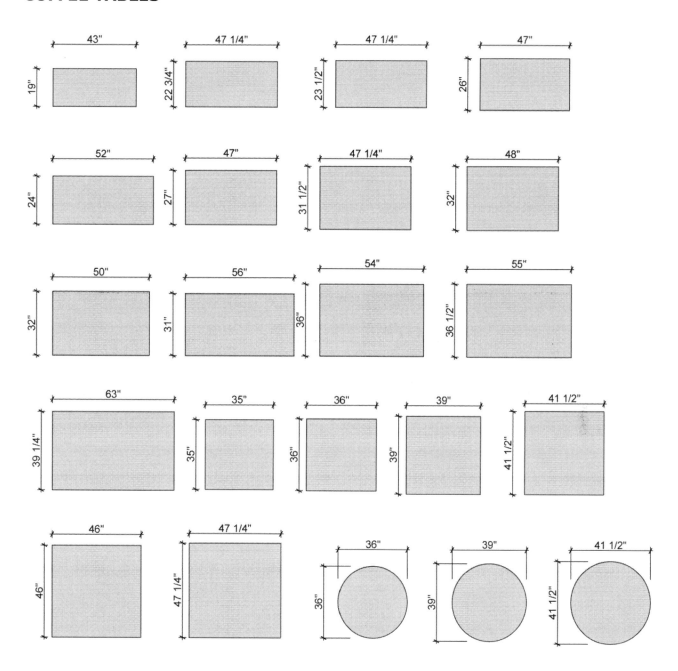

IMPERIAL / SCALE 1/4"= 1'-0"/ measurements in inches

205

CONSOLE TABLES/ENTRY HALL TABLES

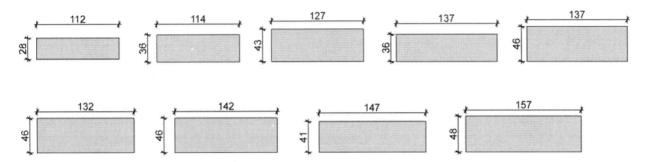

END TABLES

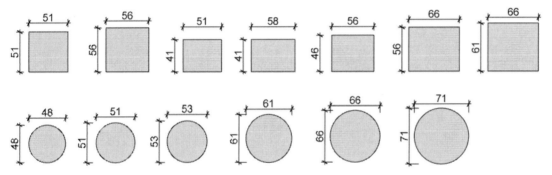

METRIC / SCALE 1:50 / measurments in cm

CONSOLE TABLES/ENTRY HALL TABLES

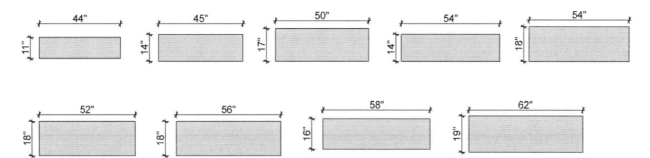

END TABLES

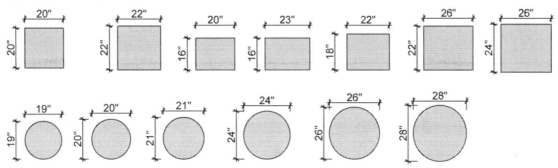

IMPERIAL / SCALE 1/4"= 1'-0"/ measurements in inches

L-SHAPED SEATING LAYOUTS/TWO SOFAS

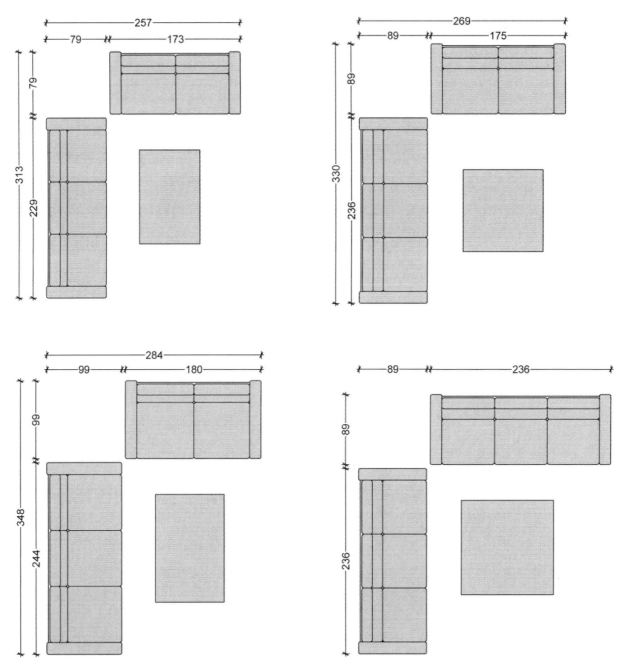

METRIC / SCALE 1:50 / measurments in cm

L-SHAPED SEATING LAYOUTS/TWO SOFAS

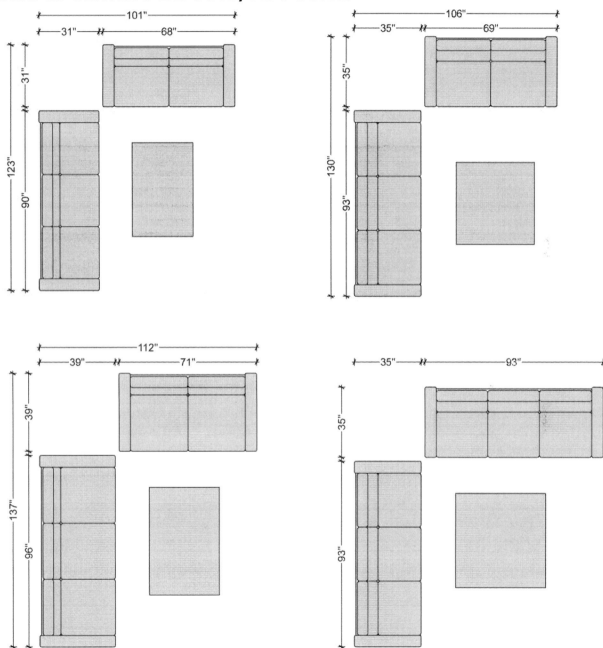

IMPERIAL / SCALE 1/4"= 1'-0"/ measurements in inches

L-SHAPED SEATING LAYOUTS/SECTIONAL SOFAS

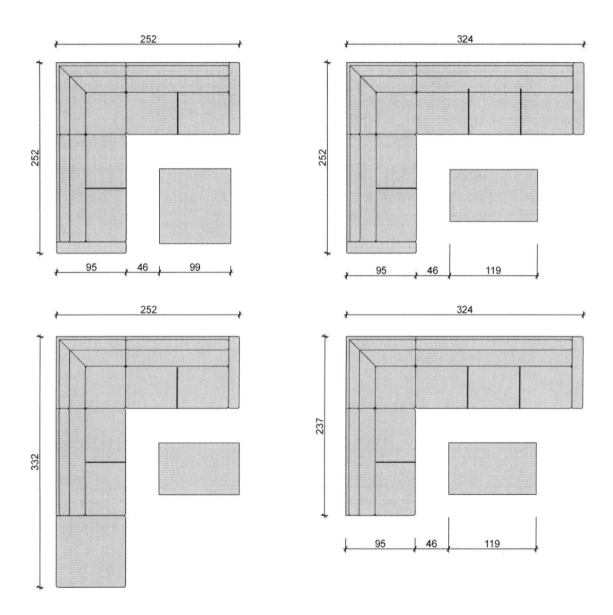

METRIC / SCALE 1:50 / measurments in cm

L-SHAPED SEATING LAYOUTS/SECTIONAL SOFAS

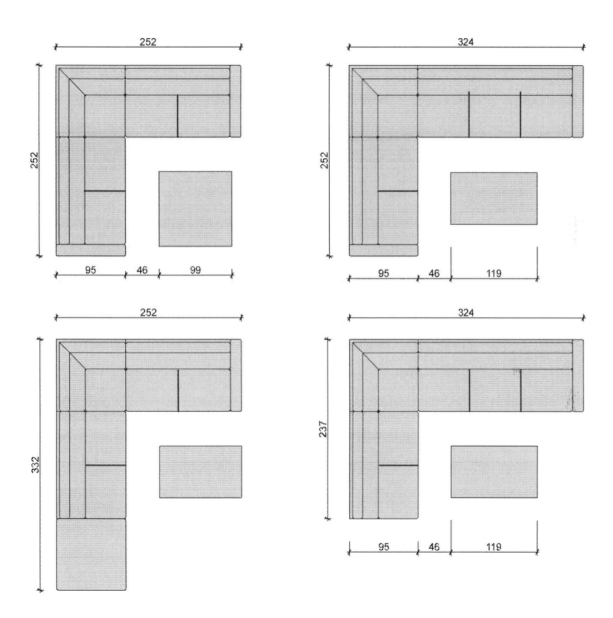

IMPERIAL / SCALE 1/4"= 1'-0"/ measurements in inches

L-SHAPED SEATING LAYOUTS/SOFA & CHAIRS

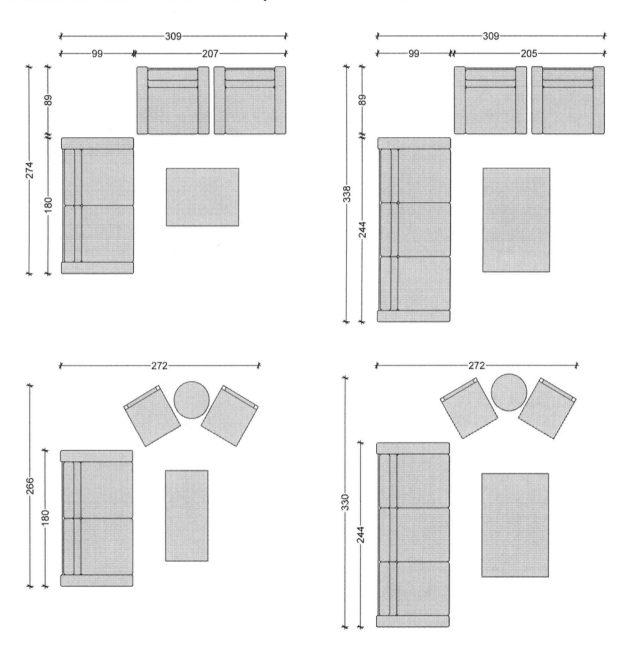

METRIC / SCALE 1:50 / measurments in cm

L-SHAPED SEATING LAYOUTS/SOFA & CHAIRS

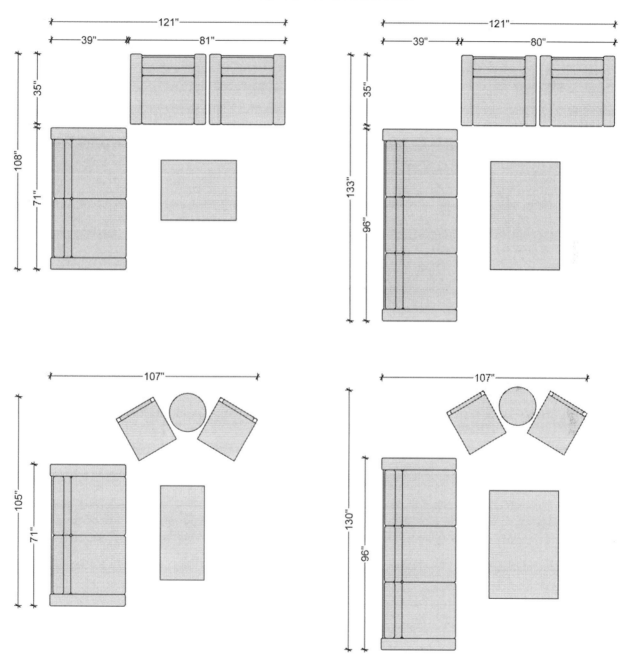

IMPERIAL / SCALE 1/4"= 1'-0"/ measurements in inches

L-SHAPED SEATING LAYOUTS/SOFA & CHAIRS

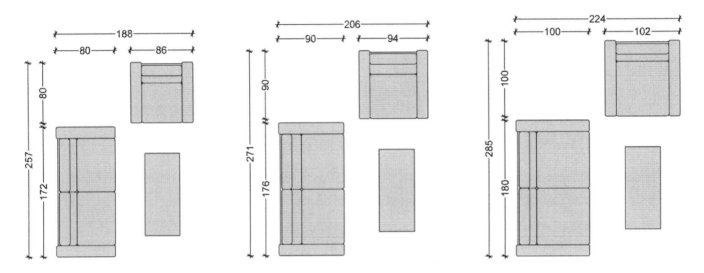

L-SHAPED SEATING LAYOUTS/SOFA & CHAISE LONGUE

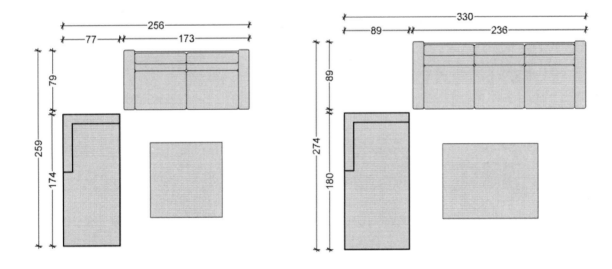

METRIC / SCALE 1:50 / measurments in cm

L-SHAPED SEATING LAYOUTS/SOFA & CHAIRS

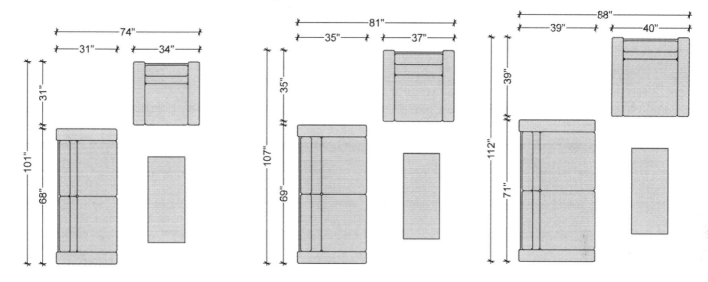

L-SHAPED SEATING LAYOUTS/SOFA & CHAISE LONGUE

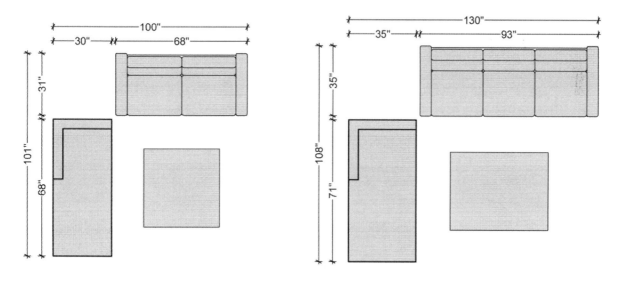

IMPERIAL / SCALE 1/4"= 1'-0"/ measurements in inches

FACE-TO-FACE SEATING LAYOUTS/SOFAS

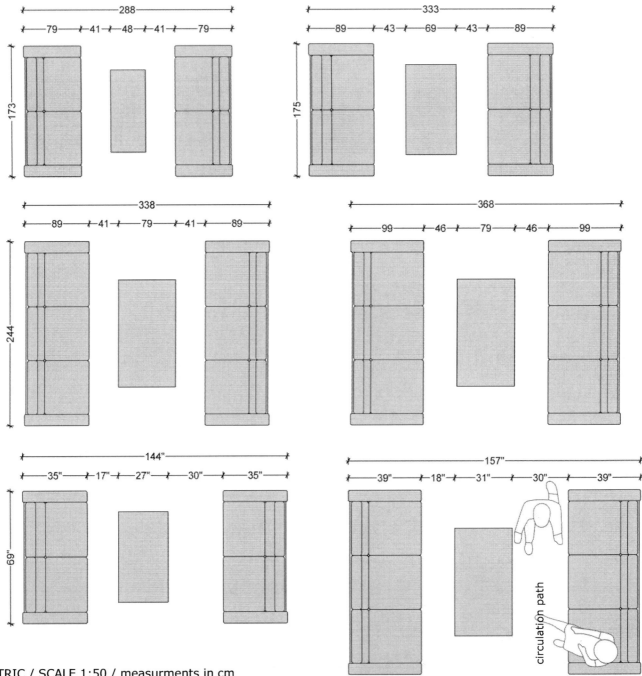

METRIC / SCALE 1:50 / measurments in cm

FACE-TO-FACE SEATING LAYOUTS/SOFAS

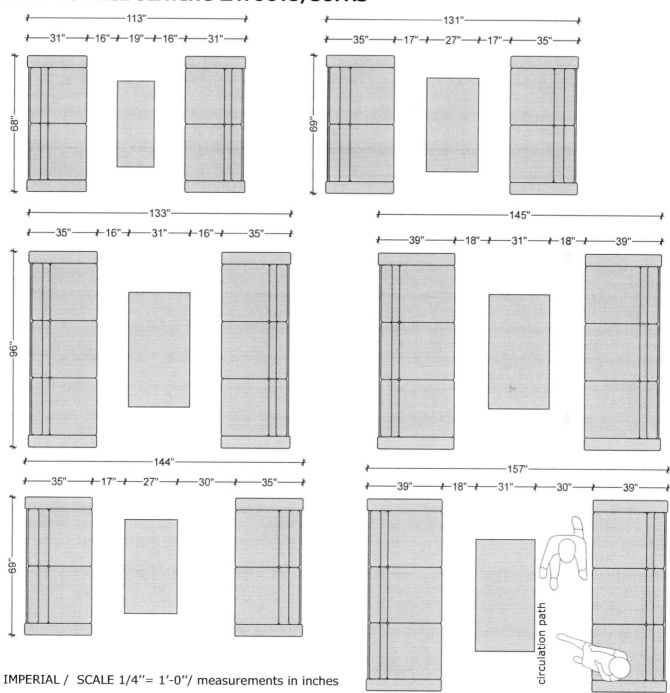

IMPERIAL / SCALE 1/4"= 1'-0"/ measurements in inches

217

U-SHAPED SEATING LAYOUTS/THREE SOFAS

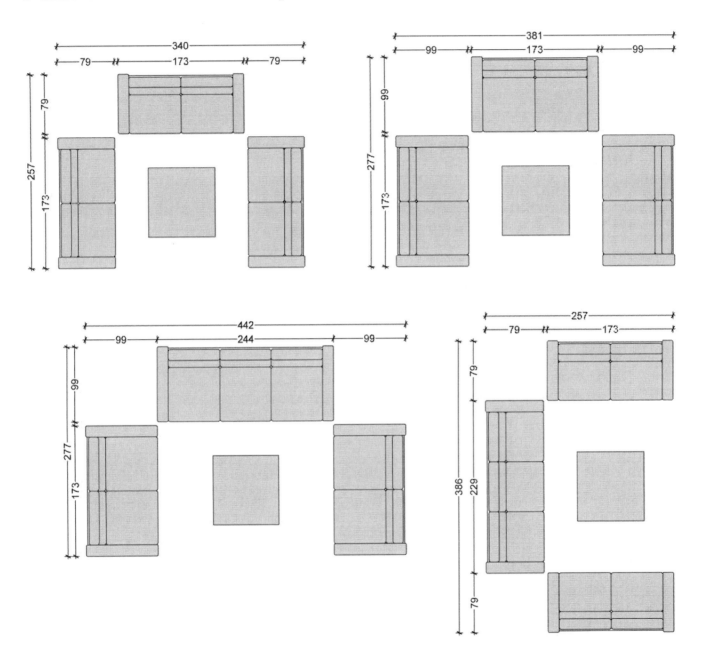

METRIC / SCALE 1:50 / measurments in cm

U-SHAPED SEATING LAYOUTS/THREE SOFAS

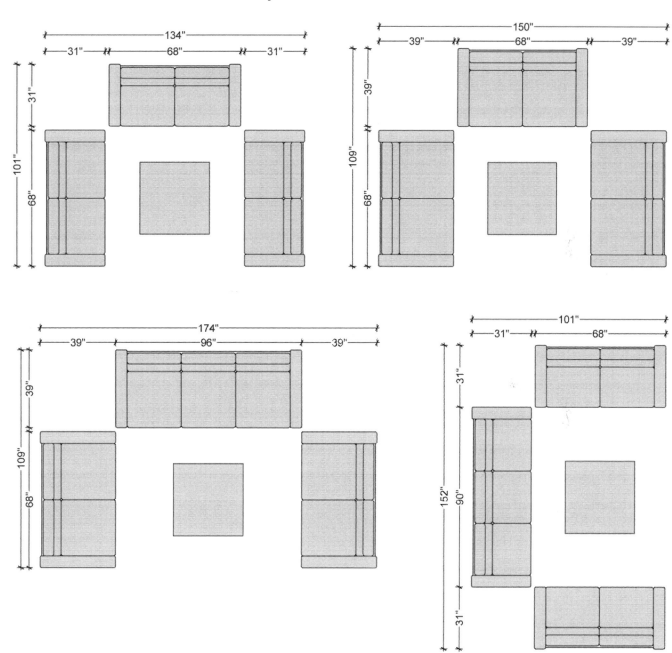

U-SHAPED SEATING LAYOUTS/SECTIONAL & SOFA

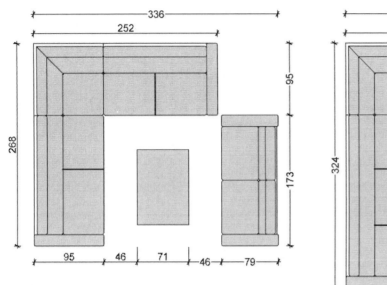

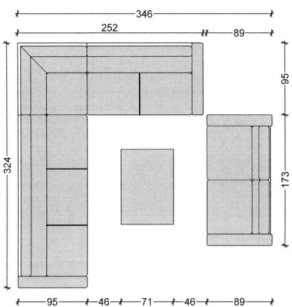

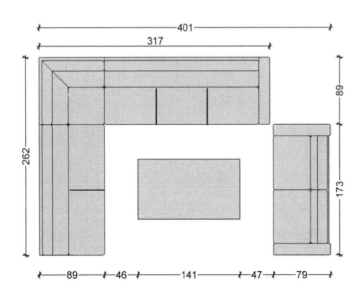

METRIC / SCALE 1:50 / measurments in cm

U-SHAPED SEATING LAYOUTS/SECTIONAL & SOFA

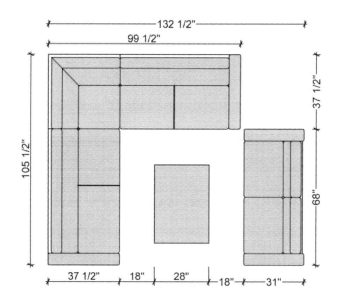

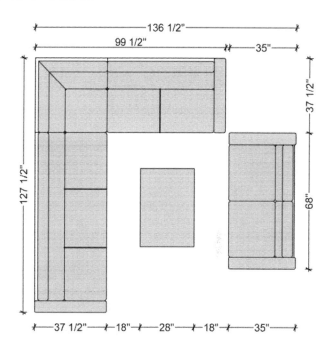

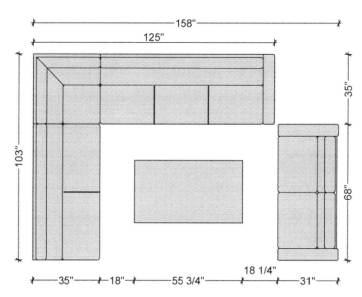

IMPERIAL / SCALE 1/4"= 1'-0"/ measurements in inches

U-SHAPED SEATING LAYOUTS/SECTIONAL & CHAIRS

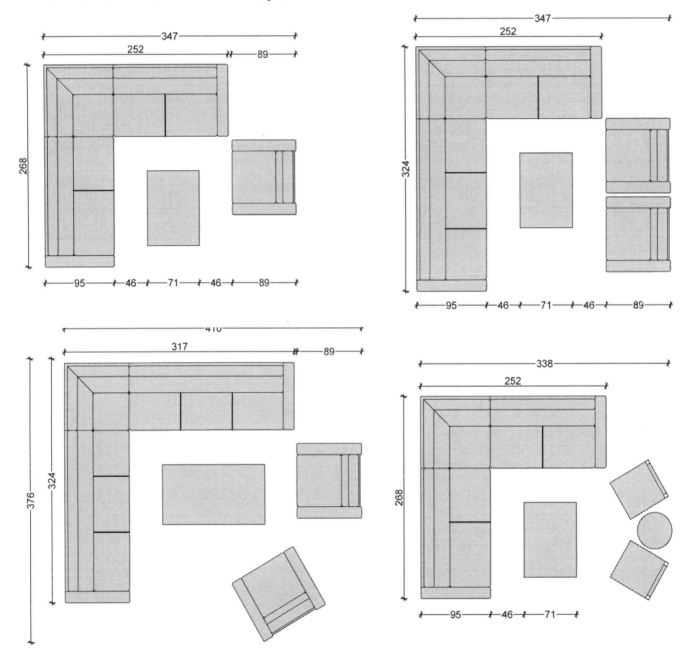

METRIC / SCALE 1:50 / measurments in cm

222

U-SHAPED SEATING LAYOUTS/SECTIONAL & CHAIRS

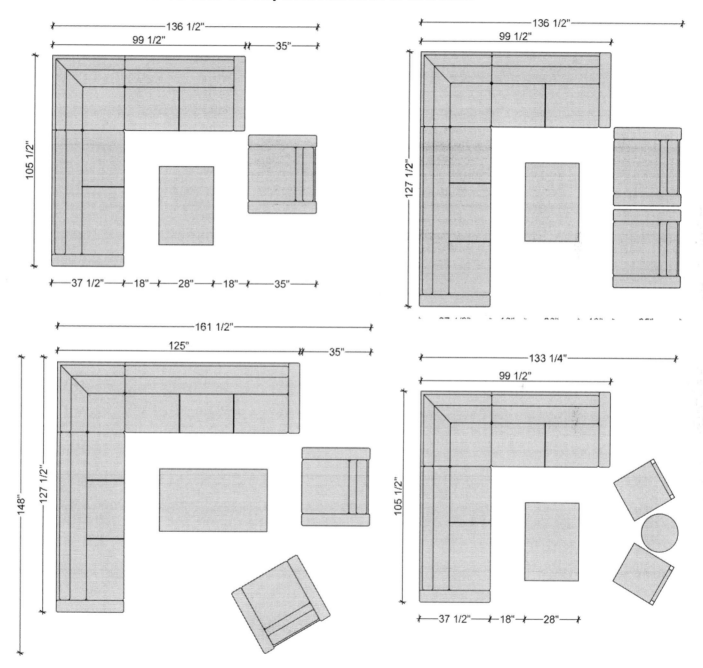

IMPERIAL / SCALE 1/4"= 1'-0"/ measurements in inches

223

U-SHAPED SEATING LAYOUTS/SOFAS & CHAIRS

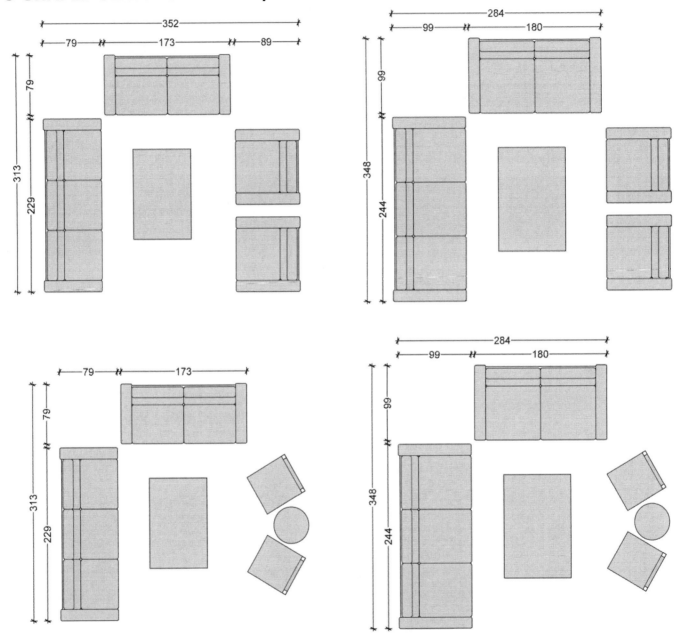

METRIC / SCALE 1:50 / measurments in cm

U-SHAPED SEATING LAYOUTS/SOFAS & CHAIRS

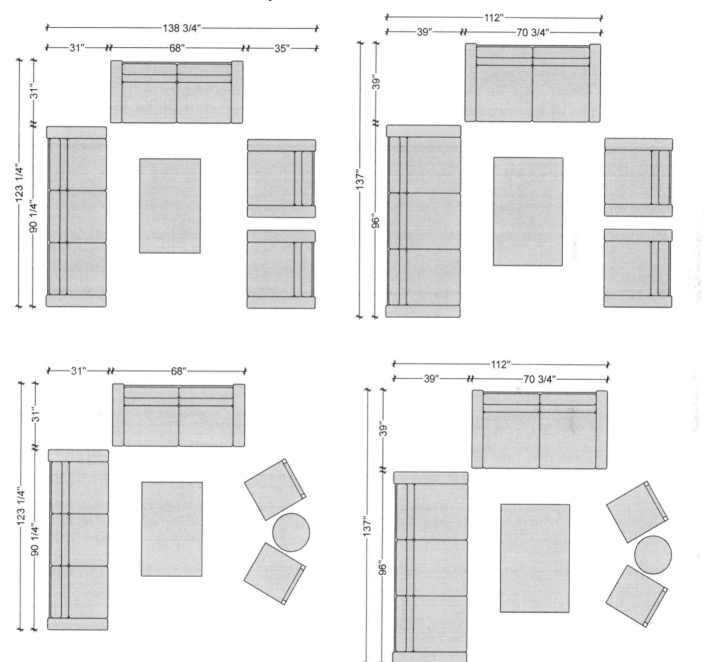

IMPERIAL / SCALE 1/4"= 1'-0"/ measurements in inches

U-SHAPED SEATING LAYOUTS/SOFA & ARMCHAIRS

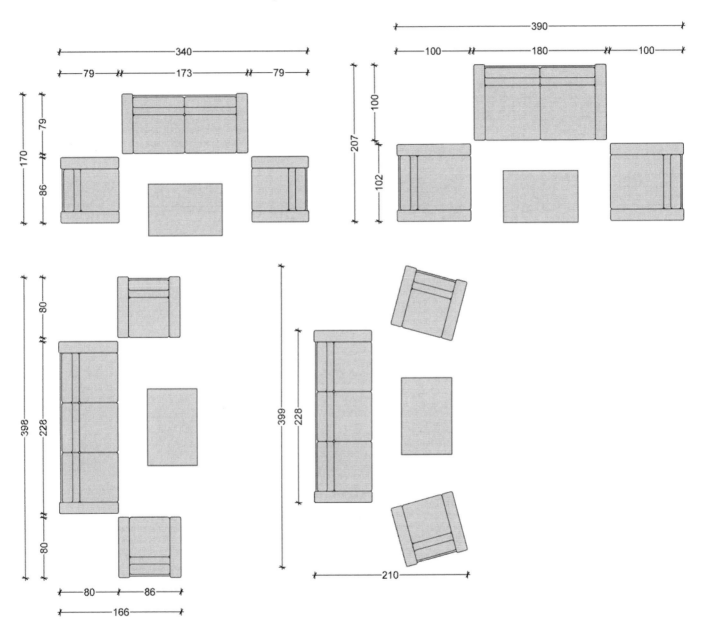

METRIC / SCALE 1:50 / measurments in cm

U-SHAPED SEATING LAYOUTS/SOFA & ARMCHAIRS

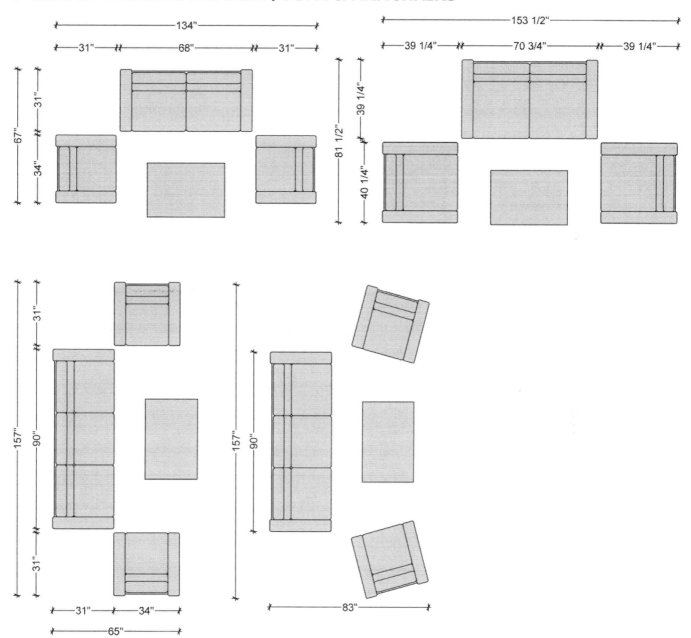

IMPERIAL / SCALE 1/4"= 1'-0"/ measurements in inches

227

CIRCULAR SEATING LAYOUTS/SOFAS, CHAIRS & OTTOMANS

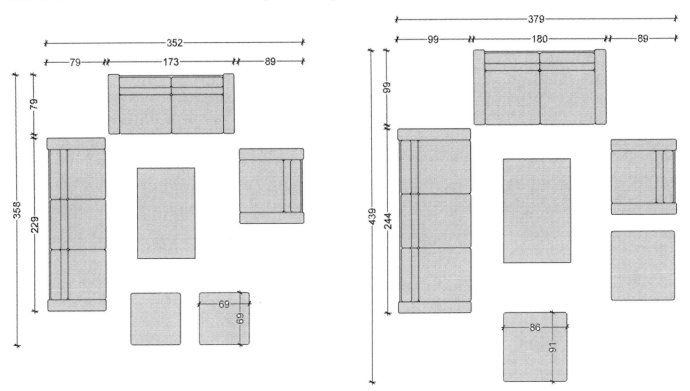

CIRCULAR SEATING LAYOUTS/CHAIRS AROUND A TABLE

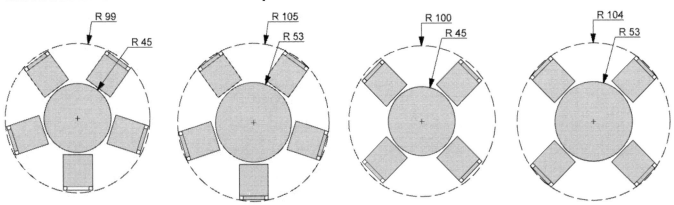

METRIC / SCALE 1:50 / measurments in cm

CIRCULAR SEATING LAYOUTS/SOFAS, CHAIRS & OTTOMANS

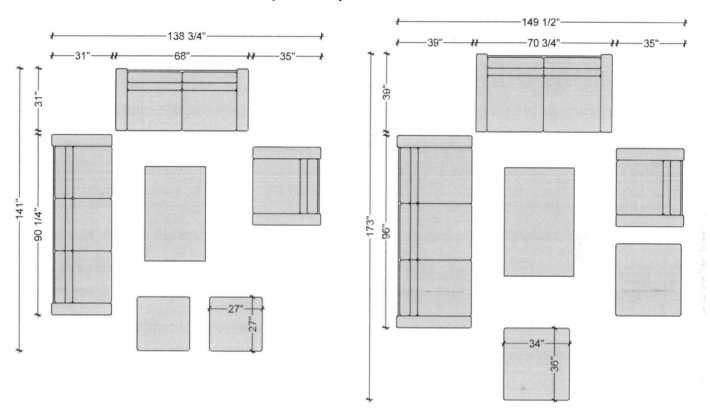

CIRCULAR SEATING LAYOUTS/CHAIRS AROUND A TABLE

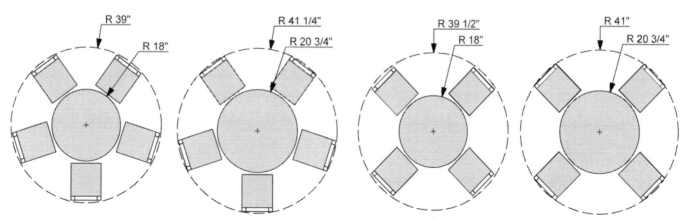

IMPERIAL / SCALE 1/4"= 1'-0"/ measurements in inches

CIRCULAR SEATING LAYOUTS/SOFAS, CHAIRS & OTTOMANS

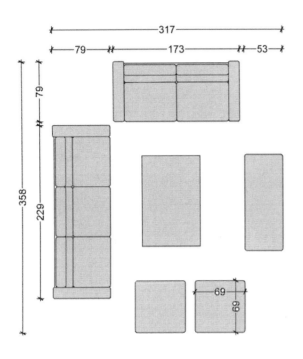

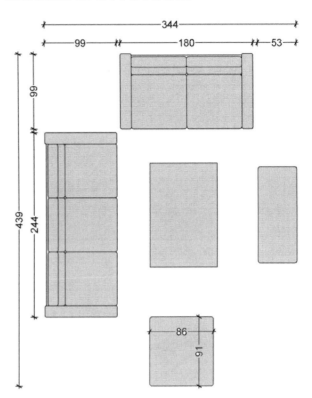

METRIC / SCALE 1:50 / measurments in cm

CIRCULAR SEATING LAYOUTS/SOFAS, BENCH & OTTOMANS

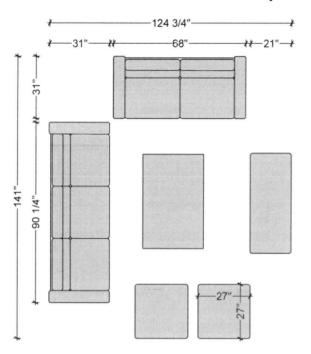

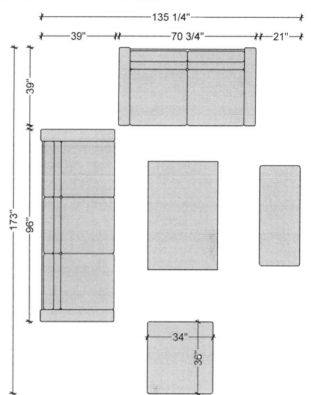

IMPERIAL / SCALE 1/4''= 1'-0''/ measurements in inches

SQUARE DINING TABLES WITH CHAIRS (and minimum clearance)

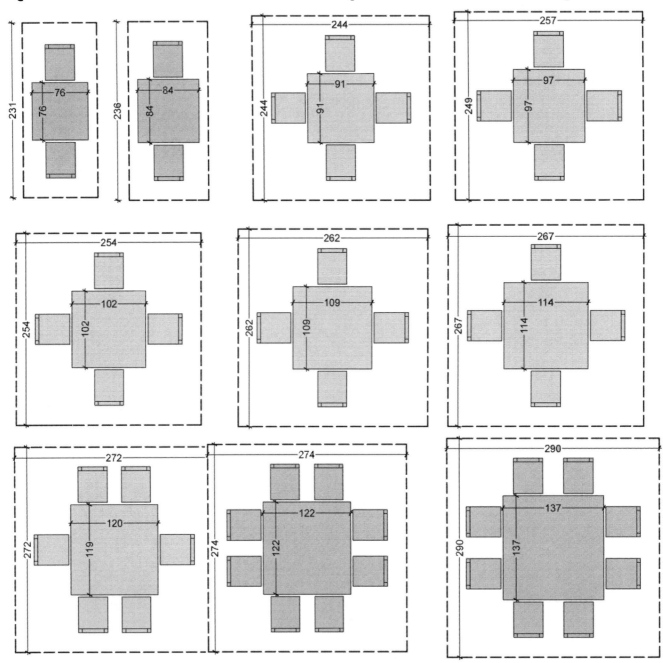

METRIC / SCALE 1:50 / measurments in cm

SQUARE DINING TABLES WITH CHAIRS (and minimum clearance)

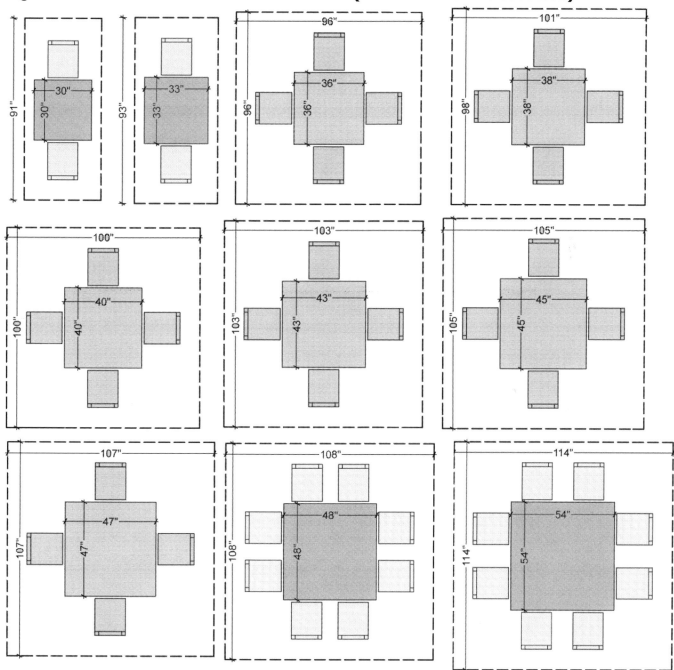

IMPERIAL / SCALE 1/4"= 1'-0"/ measurements in inches

233

RECTANGULAR DINING TABLES WITH CHAIRS (and minimum clearance)

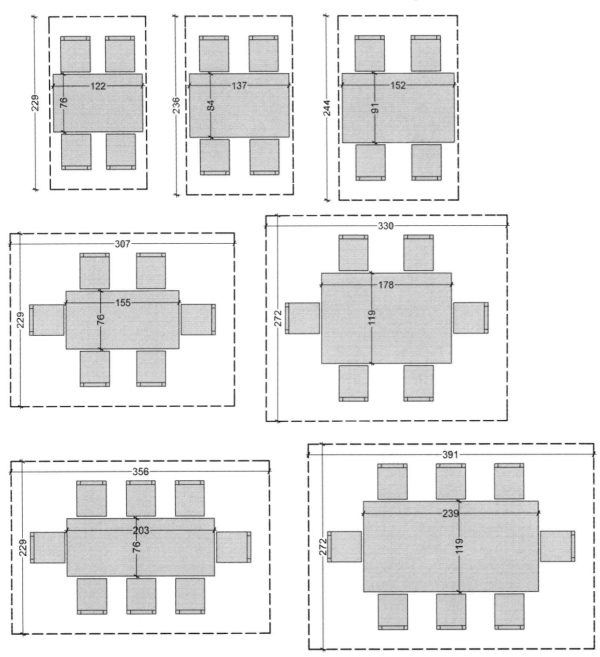

METRIC / SCALE 1:50 / measurments in cm

RECTANGULAR DINING TABLES WITH CHAIRS (and minimum clearance)

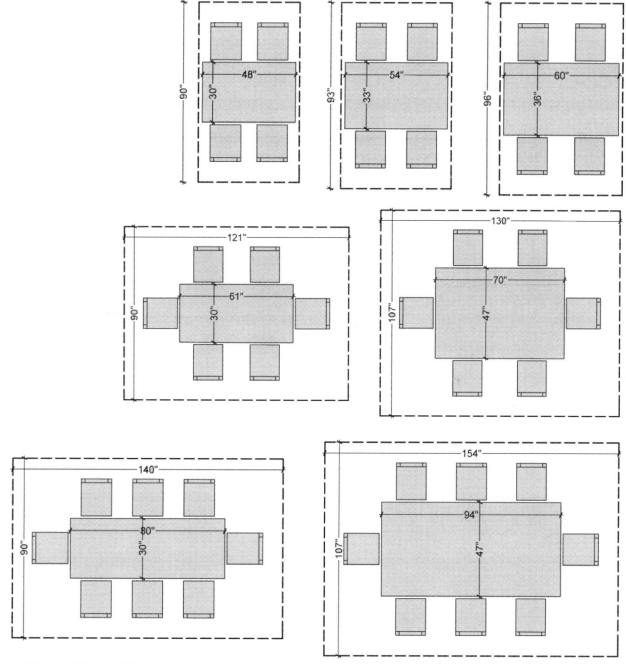

IMPERIAL / SCALE 1/4"= 1'-0"/ measurements in inches

RECTANGULAR DINING TABLES WITH CHAIRS (and minimum clearance)

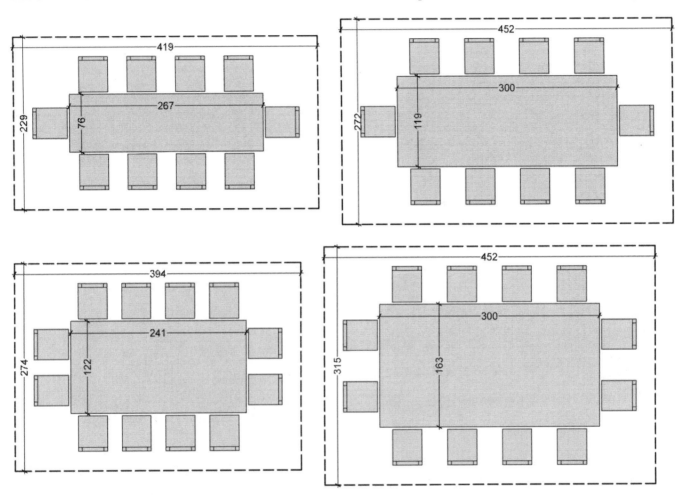

METRIC / SCALE 1:50 / measurments in cm

RECTANGULAR DINING TABLES WITH CHAIRS (and minimum clearance)

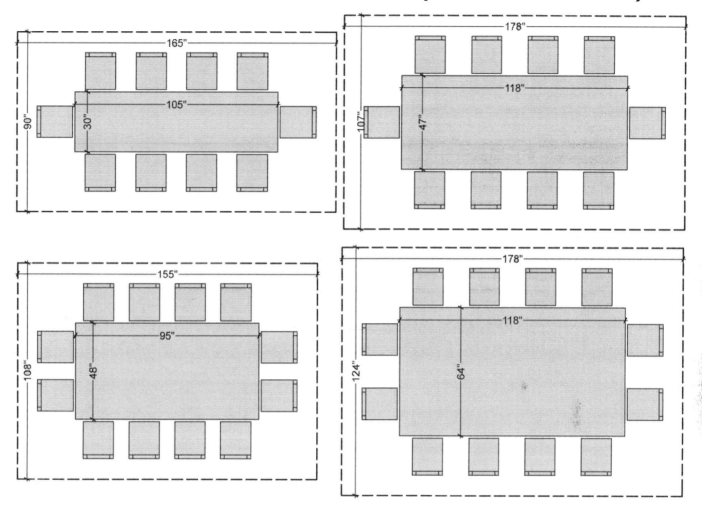

IMPERIAL / SCALE 1/4"= 1'-0"/ measurements in inches

RECTANGULAR DINING TABLES WITH CHAIRS (and minimum clearance)

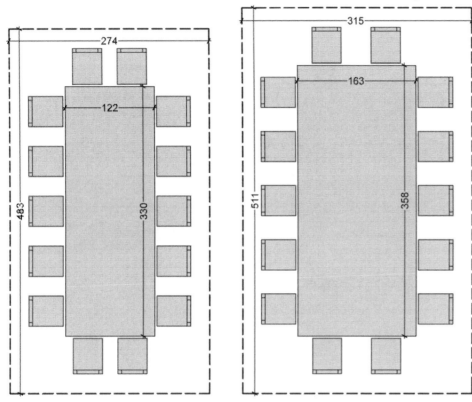

METRIC / SCALE 1:50 / measurments in cm

RECTANGULAR DINING TABLES WITH CHAIRS (and minimum clearance)

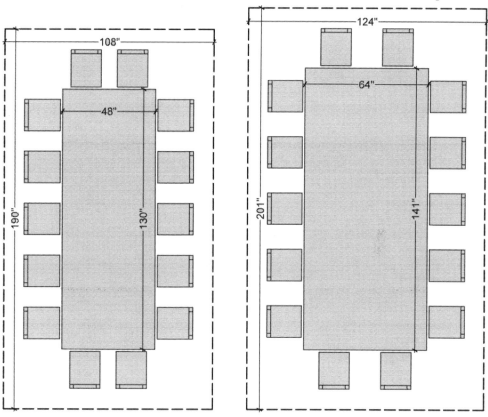

IMPERIAL / SCALE 1/4''= 1'-0''/ measurements in inches

ROUND DINING TABLES WITH CHAIRS (and minimum clearance)

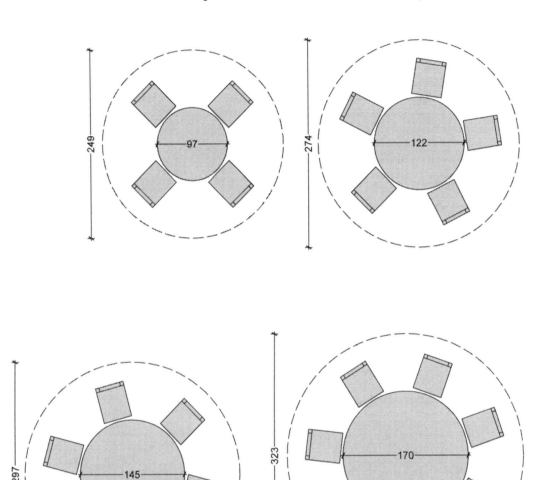

METRIC / SCALE 1:50 / measurments in cm

ROUND DINING TABLES WITH CHAIRS (and minimum clearance)

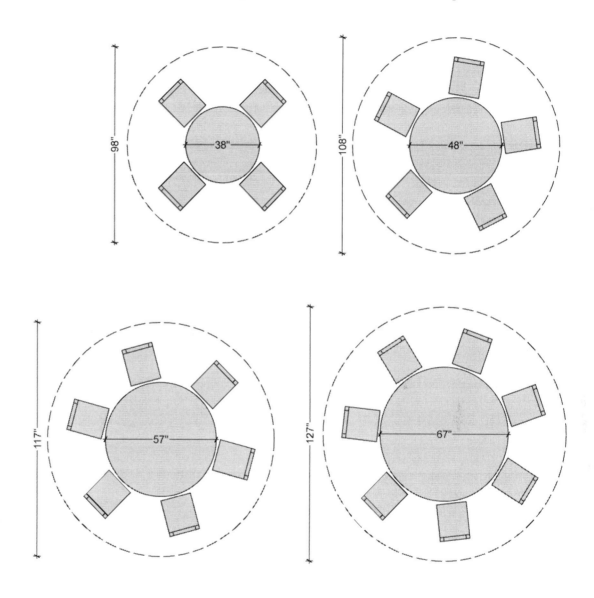

IMPERIAL / SCALE 1/4"= 1'-0"/ measurements in inches

ROUND DINING TABLES WITH CHAIRS (and minimum clearance)

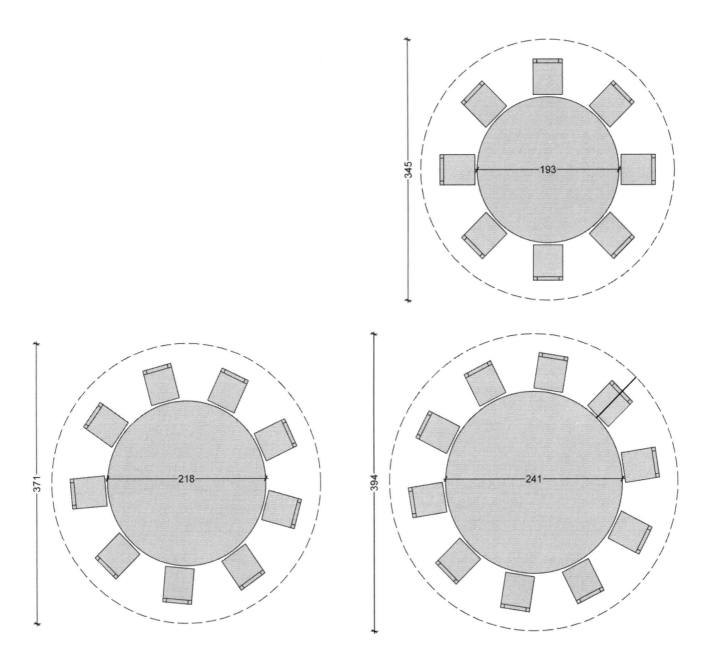

METRIC / SCALE 1:50 / measurments in cm

ROUND DINING TABLES WITH CHAIRS (and minimum clearance)

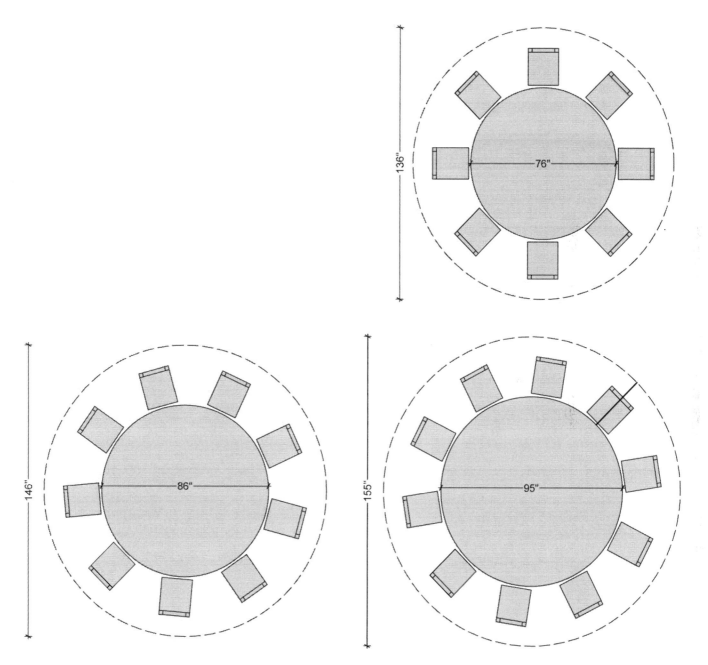

76"

136"

86"

146"

95"

155"

IMPERIAL / SCALE 1/4"= 1'-0"/ measurements in inches

OVAL DINING TABLES WITH CHAIRS (and minimum clearance)

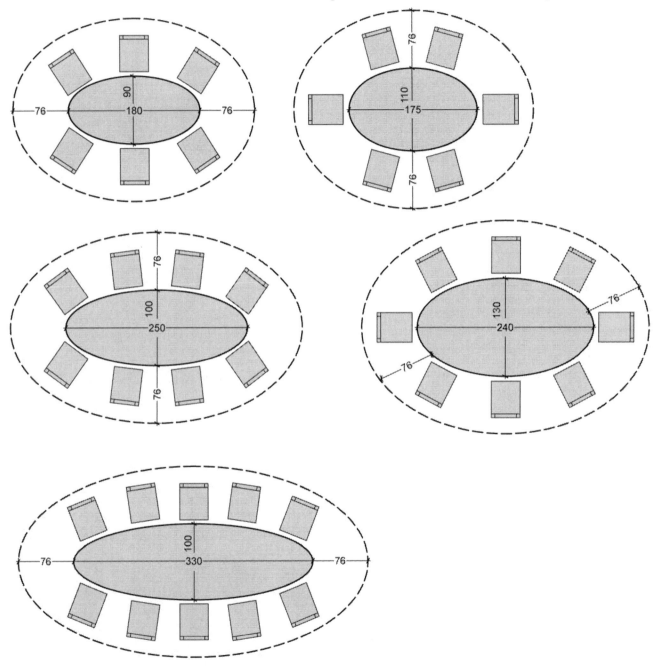

METRIC / SCALE 1:50 / measurments in cm

OVAL DINING TABLES WITH CHAIRS (and minimum clearance)

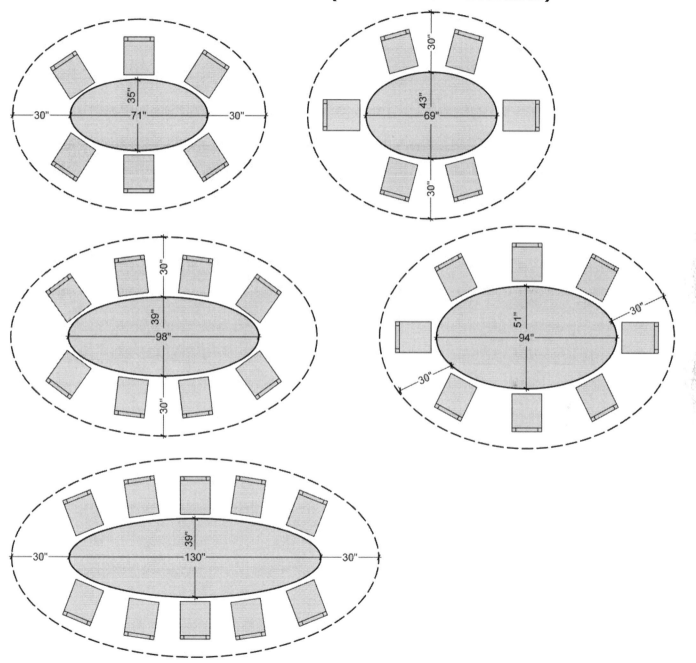

IMPERIAL / SCALE 1/4"= 1'-0"/ measurements in inches

OVAL DINING TABLES WITH CHAIRS (and minimum clearance)

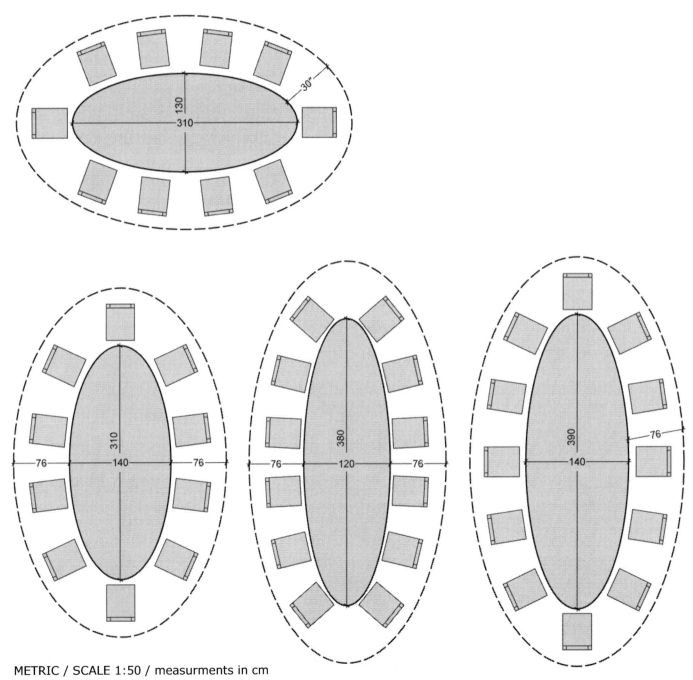

METRIC / SCALE 1:50 / measurments in cm

OVAL DINING TABLES WITH CHAIRS (and minimum clearance)

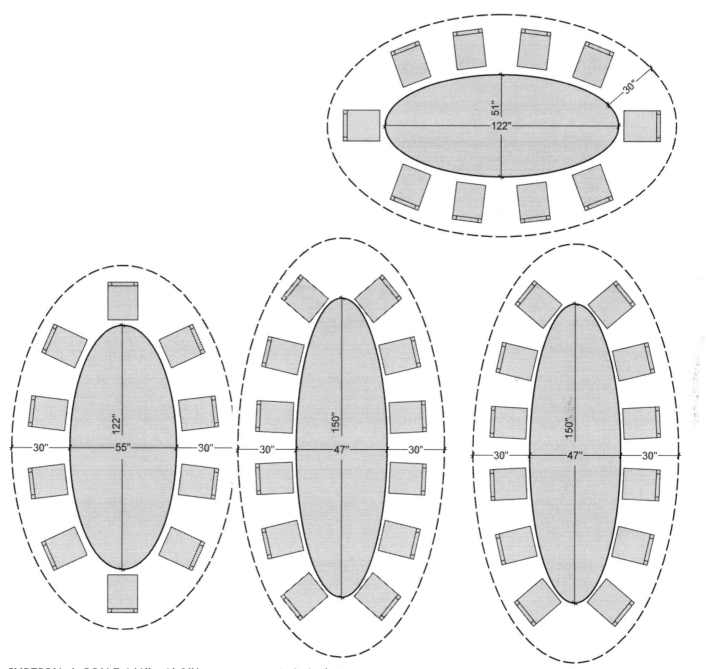

IMPERIAL / SCALE 1/4"= 1'-0"/ measurements in inches

DINING CABINETS

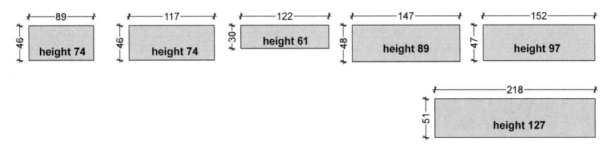

89 × 46, height 74	117 × 46, height 74
122 × 30, height 61	147 × 48, height 89
152 × 47, height 97	218 × 51, height 127

BOOKCASES

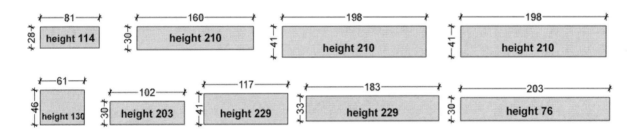

81 × 28, height 114	160 × 30, height 210
198 × 41, height 210	198 × 41, height 210
61 × 46, height 130	102 × 30, height 203
117 × 41, height 229	183 × 33, height 229
203 × 30, height 76	

METRIC / SCALE 1:50 / measurments in cm

DINING CABINETS

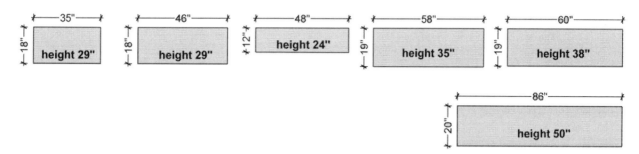

35" × 18"	height 29"
46" × 18"	height 29"
48" × 12"	height 24"
58" × 19"	height 35"
60" × 19"	height 38"
86" × 20"	height 50"

BOOKCASES

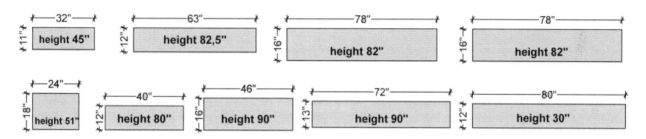

32" × 11"	height 45"
63" × 12"	height 82,5"
78" × 16"	height 82"
78" × 16"	height 82"
24" × 18"	height 51"
40" × 12"	height 80"
46" × 16"	height 90"
72" × 13"	height 90"
80" × 12"	height 30"

IMPERIAL / SCALE 1/4"= 1'-0"/ measurements in inches

USA BEDS

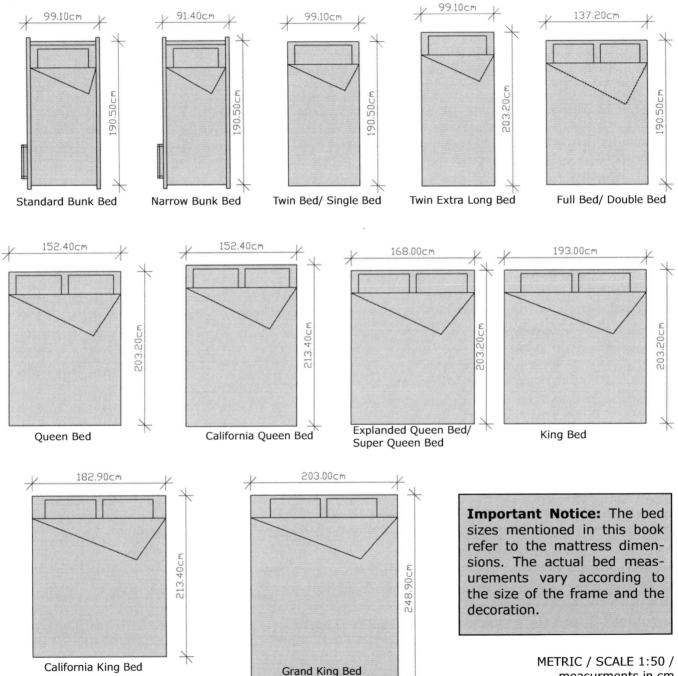

Standard Bunk Bed — 99.10cm × 190.50cm

Narrow Bunk Bed — 91.40cm × 190.50cm

Twin Bed/ Single Bed — 99.10cm × 190.50cm

Twin Extra Long Bed — 99.10cm × 203.20cm

Full Bed/ Double Bed — 137.20cm × 190.50cm

Queen Bed — 152.40cm × 203.20cm

California Queen Bed — 152.40cm × 213.40cm

Explanded Queen Bed/ Super Queen Bed — 168.00cm × 203.20cm

King Bed — 193.00cm × 203.20cm

California King Bed — 182.90cm × 213.40cm

Grand King Bed — 203.00cm × 248.90cm

Important Notice: The bed sizes mentioned in this book refer to the mattress dimensions. The actual bed measurements vary according to the size of the frame and the decoration.

METRIC / SCALE 1:50 / measurments in cm

USA BEDS

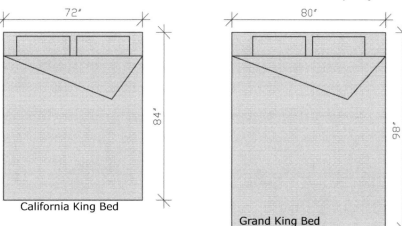

39″ / 75″	36″ / 75″	39″ / 75″	39″ / 80″	54″ / 75″
Standard Bunk Bed	Narrow Bunk Bed	Twin Bed/ Single Bed	Twin Extra Long Bed	Full Bed/ Double Bed

60″ / 80″	60″ / 84″	66″ / 80″	76″ / 80″
Queen Bed	California Queen Bed	Explanded Queen Bed/ Super Queen Bed	King Bed

72″ / 84″	80″ / 98″
California King Bed	Grand King Bed

Important Notice: The bed sizes mentioned in this book refer to the mattress dimensions. The actual bed measurements vary according to the size of the frame and the decoration.

IMPERIAL / SCALE 1/4″= 1′-0″/ measurements in inches

251

UK BEDS

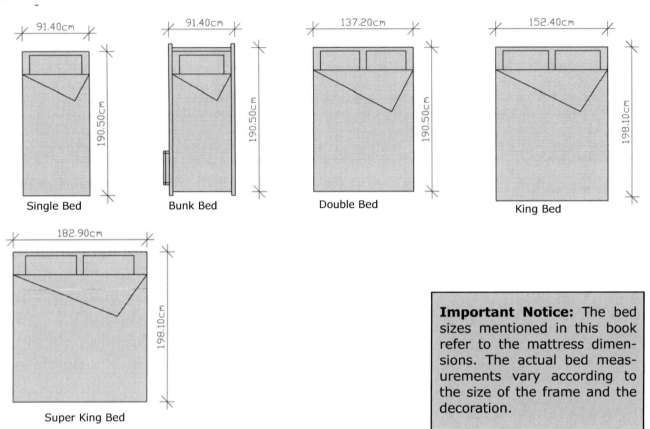

91.40cm / 190.50cm — Single Bed	91.40cm / 190.50cm — Bunk Bed
137.20cm / 190.50cm — Double Bed	152.40cm / 198.10cm — King Bed

182.90cm / 198.10cm — Super King Bed

Important Notice: The bed sizes mentioned in this book refer to the mattress dimensions. The actual bed measurements vary according to the size of the frame and the decoration.

BEDSIDE TABLES

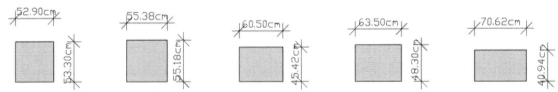

52.90cm / 53.30cm

55.38cm / 55.18cm

60.50cm / 45.42cm

63.50cm / 48.30cm

70.62cm / 40.94cm

METRIC / SCALE 1:50 / measurments in cm

UK BEDS

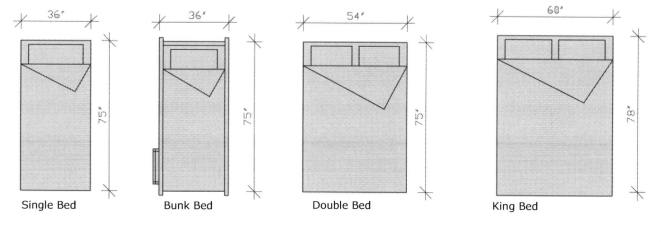

Single Bed   Bunk Bed   Double Bed   King Bed

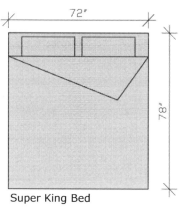

Super King Bed

Important Notice: The bed sizes mentioned in this book refer to the mattress dimensions. The actual bed measurements vary according to the size of the frame and the decoration.

BEDSIDE TABLES

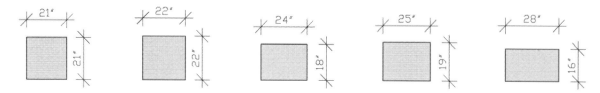

IMPERIAL / SCALE 1/4"= 1'-0"/ measurements in inches

CHANGING TABLES

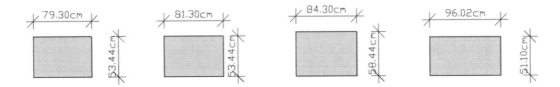

CHEST OF DRAWERS

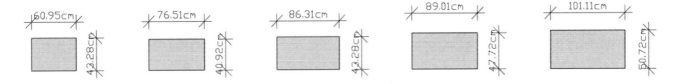

DRESSERS

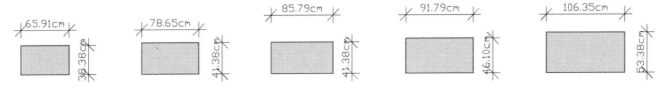

DOUBLE DRESSERS

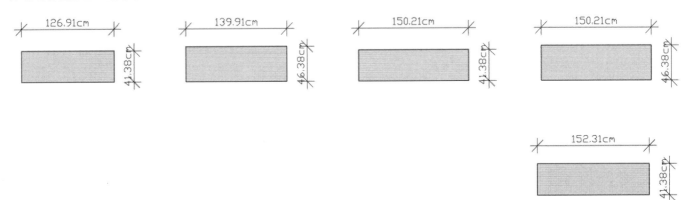

METRIC / SCALE 1:50 / measurments in cm

254

CHANGING TABLES

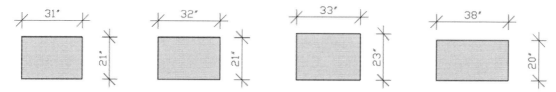

CHEST OF DRAWERS

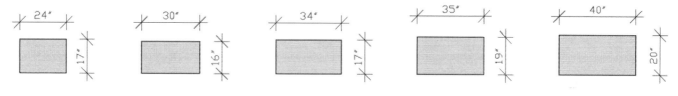

DRESSERS

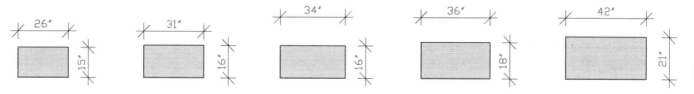

DOUBLE DRESSERS

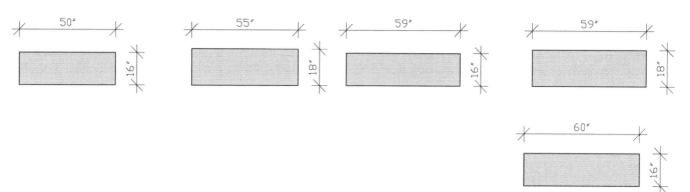

IMPERIAL / SCALE 1/4"= 1'-0"/ measurements in inches

CHILDREN'S DESKS

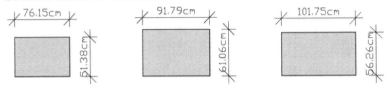

COMPUTER DESKS

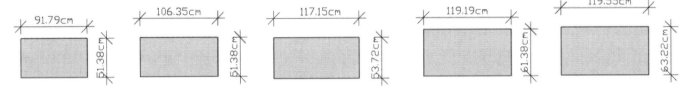

WRITING DESKS

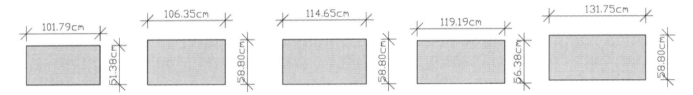

SECRETARY/SLANT FRONT DESKS

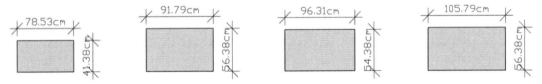

STANDING BOOKCASES

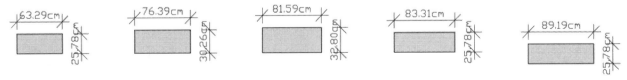

METRIC / SCALE 1:50 / measurments in cm

CHILDREN'S DESKS

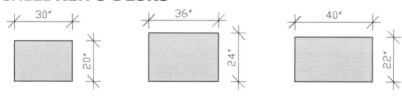

COMPUTER DESKS

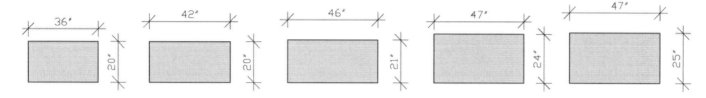

WRITING DESKS

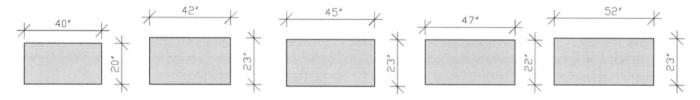

SECRETARY/SLANT FRONT DESKS

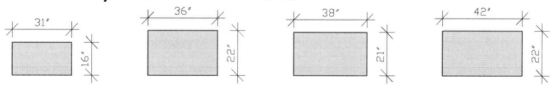

STANDING BOOKCASES

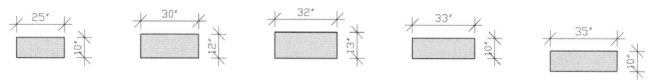

IMPERIAL / SCALE 1/4"= 1'-0"/ measurements in inches

BEDROOM VANITIES

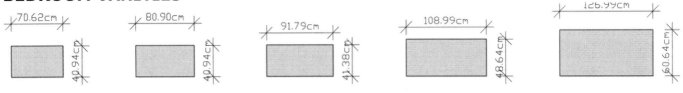

STEP BACK CABINETS

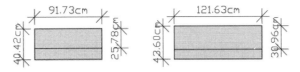

HANGING SHELVES

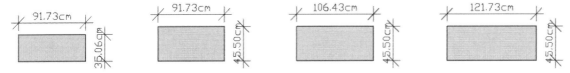

ADULTS DESK CHAIRS

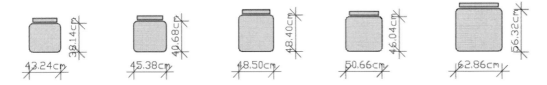

ELEMENTARY SCHOOL AGE CHILDREN'S CHAIRS

METRIC / SCALE 1:50 / measurments in cm

BEDROOM VANITIES

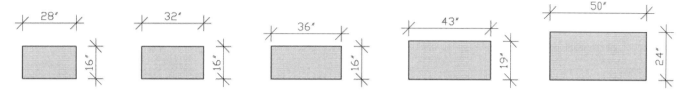

STEP BACK CABINETS

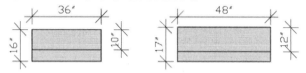

HANGING SHELVES

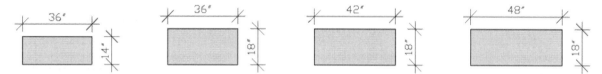

ADULTS DESK CHAIRS

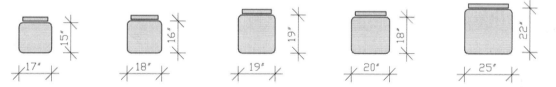

ELEMENTARY SCHOOL AGE CHILDREN'S CHAIRS

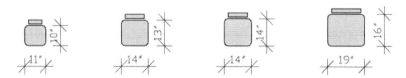

IMPERIAL / SCALE 1/4"= 1'-0"/ measurements in inches

BASSINETS

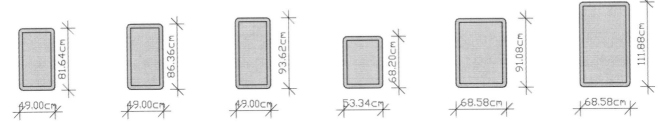

CRANDLES

PLAYPENS

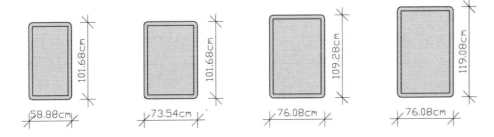

JUNIOR CRIBS

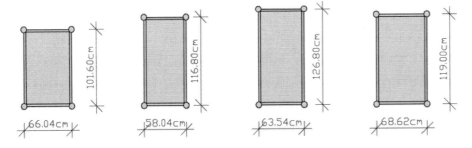

METRIC / SCALE 1:50 / measurments in cm

BASSINETS

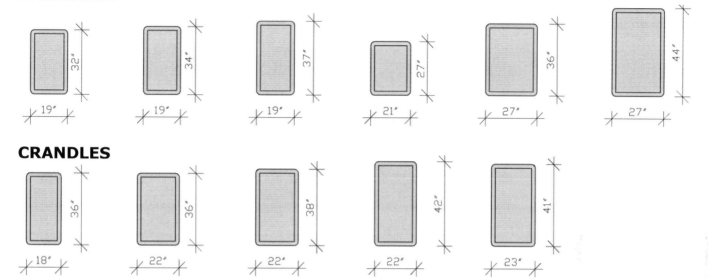

CRANDLES

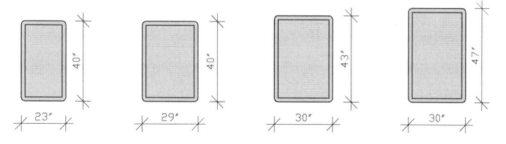

PLAYPENS

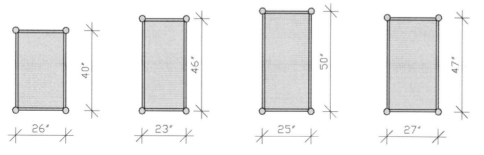

JUNIOR CRIBS

IMPERIAL / SCALE 1/4"= 1'-0"/ measurements in inches

261

6-YEAR CRIBS

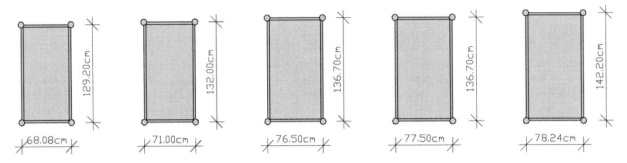

129.20cm
68.08cm

132.00cm
71.00cm

136.70cm
76.50cm

136.70cm
77.50cm

142.20cm
78.24cm

YOUTH BEDS

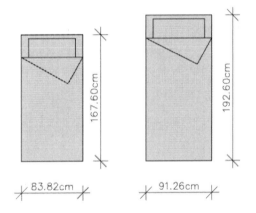

167.60cm
83.82cm

192.60cm
91.26cm

METRIC / SCALE 1:50 / measurments in cm

6-YEAR CRIBS

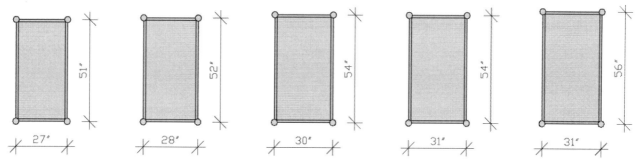

51" 27"
52" 28"
54" 30"
54" 31"
56" 31"

YOUTH BEDS

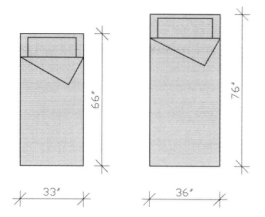

66" 33"
76" 36"

IMPERIAL / SCALE 1/4"= 1'-0"/ measurements in inches

II. GRAPH PAPERS

IIIIIIIIIIIIIIIIIIIIIIIIIIIIIIIIIIIIII
IIIIIIIIIIIIIIIIIIIIIIIIIIIIIIIIIIIIII
IIIIIIIIIIIIIIIIIIIIIIIIIIIIIIIIIIIIIII

Appendix II: Graph paper

The graph papers are in scale. So, in case you print them do not enlarge or reduce the pages. Simple photocopy them keeping the scale same.

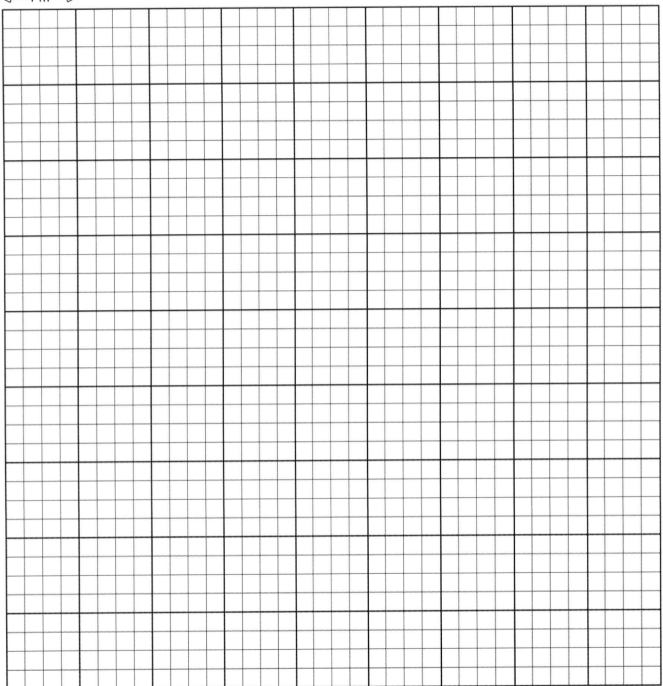

1 foot

1 foot

Bibliography

Corky Binggeli, 2011. Interior Graphic Standards: Student Edition (Ramsey/Sleeper Architectural Graphic Standards Series). 2 Edition. Wiley.

Ernst Neufert, 2012. Neufert Architects' Data, Fourth Edition. 4 Edition. Wiley-Blackwell.

Julius Panero, 1979. Human Dimension & Interior Space: A Source Book of Design Reference Standards. First Printing Edition. Watson-Guptill

Julius Panero, and Martin Zelnik Joesph DeChiara, 2001. Interior Design and Space Planning (Time-Saver standards for Interior Design and Space Planning second edition). 2nd Edition. McGraw Hill.

Roberto J. Rengel, 2011. The Interior Plan: Concepts and Exercises. 1 Edition. Fairchild Books.

S.C. Reznikoff, 1986. Interior Graphic and Design Standards. Edition. Watson-Guptill.

About the authors

V. Asaroglou is an architect. She retains an architectural studio in Thessaloniki, Greece undertaking residential and commercial projects and interior design as well, for more than 25 years. She has taught freehand and architectural drawing to applicants to Departments of Architecture and teaches interior architectural design at Akto College (by Middlesex University). She has awarded in both art and architecture competitions, while her work has been published in books and publications.

A. Bonarou is an architect with a master of arts in education. She has taught architectural drawing, both by hand and digital media, at Akto college (by Middlesex University), as well as at the Technological Educational Institute of Serres (Department on Interior Architecture). She also works as an architecture writer, publishing articles in relevant magazines and books.

index

Printed in Great Britain
by Amazon